Shaping the Moral Life

An Approach to Moral Theology

Shaping the Moral Life

An Approach to Moral Theology

KLAUS DEMMER, M.S.C.

Edited by
JAMES F. KEENAN, S.J.

Translated by
ROBERTO DELL'ORO

With a Foreword by
THOMAS KOPFENSTEINER

GEORGETOWN UNIVERSITY PRESS / WASHINGTON, D.C.

Georgetown University Press, Washington, D.C.
© 2000 by Georgetown University Press. All rights reserved.
Printed in the United States of America

10 9 8 7 6 5 4 3 2 1   2000

This volume is printed on acid-free offset book paper.

Library of Congress Cataloging-in-Publication Data

Demmer, Klaus, 1931-
    [Introduzione alla teologia morale. English]
    Shaping the moral life : an approach to moral theology / Klaus Demmer ; translated
by Roberto Dell'Oro ; edited by James F. Keenan.
        p. cm.—(Moral traditions and moral arguments series)
    Includes bibliographical references.
    ISBN 0-87840-790-1 (alk. paper)—ISBN 0-87840-791-X (pbk. : alk. paper)
    1. Christian ethics—Catholic authors. I. Keenan, James F. II. title. III. Moral
traditions & moral arguments

BJ1249.D43 2000
241'.043—dc21   00-027255

Contents

CHAPTER THREE
THE DECISIVE FACTOR:
TOWARD A THEOLOGY OF CONSCIENCE

CHAPTER FOUR
THE MEDIATION OF FAITH AND MORAL REASON

CHAPTER FIVE
THE ECCLESIAL DIMENSION OF CHRISTIAN MORALITY

CHAPTER SIX
THE MORAL NATURAL LAW AS A BASIS OF UNIVERSAL
COMMUNICATION

CHAPTER SEVEN
THE MORAL COMMUNITY OF COMMUNICATION
AND ITS NORMS

CHAPTER EIGHT
THE JOURNEY OF MORAL DECISION

CHAPTER NINE
LIFE HISTORY AS SUFFERED AND
RECONCILED CONFLICT

CHAPTER TEN
MORAL TRUTH IN THE OPENNESS OF THE SPIRIT

CHAPTER ELEVEN
BEYOND THE HUMAN SCIENCES

CHAPTER TWELVE
RESPONSIBILITY FOR RIGHTS AND THE LAW

Editor's Note

Since 1987, I have wanted to see the moral theological writings of Klaus Demmer in English. With nearly twenty books to his credit, Demmer is one of the most formidable contributors to the field in continental Europe. Although he has published occasional essays in English, French, and Italian, 95 percent of his published writings are in German.

After speaking with Thomas Kopfensteiner, I decided that the best introduction to Demmer would be Demmer's own Italian work, *Introduzione alla Teologia Morale* (Casale Monferrato: Piemme, 1993). Demmer's work was part of a series (*Introduzione alle discipline teologiche*) of fifteen volumes authored by Gregorian University professors and designed to introduce readers to the various theological disciplines.

Later, I asked Roberto Dell'Oro of Georgetown University's Center of Clinical Ethics to translate Demmer's work into English. Like Kopfensteiner and myself, Dell'Oro had studied in Rome with Demmer. He agreed to do the translation but reminded me that Demmer originally wrote the book in German and that the Piemme publishers translated Demmer's manuscript into Italian. After contacting Demmer, Dell'Oro began the translation from Demmer's original, unpublished manuscript, *Einführung in die Moraltheologie.*

To introduce the English-speaking reader to Demmer, I invited Kopfensteiner to write the foreword and two of my students, Laura Richter and Andreas Cremer, to assemble a complete bibliography of Demmer's writings.

I know I speak for Dell'Oro and Kopfensteiner, as well as John Samples of Georgetown University Press, when I say that we believe you will find in these pages the foundational insights of an important, original thinker who engages a variety of other writers in an ongoing dialogue about ethics, the theological tradition, and hermeneutics. Through this introduction, we hope that you too will enter into the dialogue.

James F. Keenan, S.J.
Editor

Foreword

Klaus Demmer was born in 1931 in Münster, in the state of Nordrhein-Westfalen on the western border of Germany. He is a religious priest of the Missionaries of the Sacred Heart of Jesus. He studied at the Gregorian University in Rome; there, in 1961 (under Josef Fuchs, S.J.), he wrote his doctoral dissertation, *Jus caritatis*—which dealt with the Christological foundation of the natural moral law in Augustine. In 1970, after his *Habilitation* at the University of Innsbruck, he began to lecture at the Gregorian University. His tenure there continues, in the effective history of so many distinguished moral theologians of this century: Arthur Vermeersch, S.J.; Franz Hürth, S.J.; Édouard Hamel, S.J.; and, of course, Fuchs. Because of Demmer's background as a student and professor in Rome, his lectures, seminars, and publications reflect in a unique way the Second Vatican Council's vision to renew moral theology.

More than any continental moral theologian today, Demmer has transformed the neo-Scholastic patrimony by bringing it into conversation with transcendental philosophy (*Sein und Gebot*, 1971; *Die Lebensentscheidung*, 1974), the hermeneutical sciences (*Sittlich handeln aus Verstehen*, 1980), and contemporary trends in the philosophy of science (*Deuten und handeln*, 1985; *Moraltheologische Methodenlehre*, 1989). Demmer has written and lectured on all of the major topics in moral theology today—including faith and reason, the *proprium* of Christian ethics, the use of Scripture, person and nature, the role of the magisterium, the dialogue with the other sciences, norms, and the analysis of moral action. He has done so, however, with original and unparalleled insight, often providing the requisite context in which to rethink and advance many current debates.

Demmer is a *fundamental* moral theologian, which means that he is engaged in two related tasks. The first task is to establish and justify a normative theory. In the wake of the collapse of the modern project, the moral claim cannot be conceived as a law imposed upon us arbitrarily by an external authority. Instead, for Demmer the moral norm is based on our limited and fallible ability to reason, which finds itself confronting the task of realizing freedom in the world. The second task concerns the genesis of insights into goods and values and the justification of moral judgments. Demmer moves away from the truncated act-centered morality that dominated the neo-Scholastic manuals of moral theology. His concern is to show how our actions embody and carry out a more original anthropological project. Not only does this anthropological project condition our insights into goods and values, it provides the criteria by which our actions are judged morally.

Because Demmer is a fundamental *moral* theologian, his work, of course, is not detached from the questions raised in other areas of the moral enterprise. Demmer's concerns have extended beyond fundamental moral theology to include issues in bioethics (*Leben in Menschenhand*, 1987), spirituality and morality (*Gebet, das zur Tat wird*, 1989), the issue of celibacy (*Zumutung aus dem Ewigen*, 1991), and the relationship between law and morality (*Christliche Existenz unter dem Anspruch des Rechts*, 1995). There is, then, a dynamism to Demmer's work that reflects his status as a true systematic thinker. On the one hand, Demmer's research has shown that special questions are integral to the work of the fundamental moral theologian. Without them, moral theology remains sterile. On the other hand, special questions cannot be detached from the interests of the fundamental moral theologian. If they were, moral argumentation would be no more than a dangerous ideology.

Above all, Demmer is a fundamental moral *theologian.* For Demmer, moral theology is a science of faith (*Die Wahrheit leben*, 1991; *Gottes Anspruch denken*, 1993). For Demmer, the question of God is not ancillary to the moral enterprise; rather, God's revelation in Jesus Christ reveals our true identity and nature. A theological anthropology allows Demmer to conceive of revelation in an anthropological key and to interpret anthropology in a Christological key. In Demmer's theological anthropology, faith is constitutive of our identities; it is the most profound basis for our actions. Demmer does not deal with an abstract human nature; he begins with the experience of ourselves *as* believers. In this way, his work is inspired by the Augustinian adage that God is closer to us than we are to ourselves. This way of proceeding, of course, does not diminish the need for rational argumentation. Instead, by justifying our actions, we will ultimately reveal the feasibility and communicability of faith's insights.

It has been remarked that reading Demmer is like reading several authors at the same time. Demmer's writing is synthetic and reflects an incomparable distillation of ideas, schools, and thinkers. In its scope and nuance, Demmer's work eschews any attempt to isolate and to raise any one theme or issue as paradigmatic. His writings are like a web of intricately connected underground tunnels that lead an explorer deeper and deeper into an ever-expanding world. When the network of tunnels has been mapped, the explorer sees that no one part can be isolated from the whole, and the whole can be accessed through any number of individual parts. This richness and diversity engages a wide range of conversation partners, extending beyond the often too-narrow confines of moral theology to include the broader theological community and practitioners of the other sciences. Demmer's work demonstrates an appreciation for the autonomy of the other sciences without abandoning the uniqueness of the moral enterprise.

Demmer is not unknown to moral theologians in the United States. He has been a guest professor at San Francisco and Notre Dame; he also has participated in seminars and lectured in Washington, D.C. Because so little of his work is available in English, however, he is better known in Europe and elsewhere. His influence is visible in the international character of his students who contributed to the two *Festschriften* (collections published in his honor), *Ethische Theorie praktisch* and *Ethik zwischen Anspruch und Zuspruch*. To be sure, this present text will make Demmer's thought accessible to theologians and others in an unprecedented way. Demmer's students, in particular, will welcome this introduction in English and recall the lectures and seminars of which they were privileged to be a part. They will recall not only what they learned but, more important, they will remember his meekness and humility, his warm, kind, and generous heart—which, perhaps, is the best instructor in the moral life.

Thomas Kopfensteiner
Fordham University, New York

Introduction

The study of moral theology often is a problem for the interested person. The reasons for this situation are many and various. The first undeniably has to do with the increasing complexity of the field itself. At this level, moral theology shares the fate of all other scientific disciplines: Questions multiply because it has become more difficult to grasp the many facets of our life. It is not surprising that students may fail to achieve a comprehensive grasp of the subject matter; therefore, it is essential to provide them with an introduction that serves as a path in the thicket of the field. This introduction represents a starting point for students of moral theology; its goal is to sustain their efforts and focus their attention on the main theoretical issues.

The multiplication of problems is not the only source of difficulties, however. There are different ways to do moral theology and to understand its status as a science of faith in relation to the Church. Indeed, the public image of this theological discipline is anything but homogeneous, and one can hardly find unanimity. It is not wrong to speak of a pluralism of theologies; our discipline more acutely reflects this situation, for it is the closest to life. As a result, one can find different styles of thought grounded in quite different philosophical starting points. Anyone who wants to study moral theology today must be equipped with a profound philosophical culture. Some students of moral theology may find the task disconcerting, however, because the necessary philosophical preparation is quite difficult!

The aforementioned difficulties should not lead to an attitude of resignation; on the contrary, they should be taken up by all theological disciplines as their central challenge. Situations of crisis can also generate some good. One can only desire that theology students will become aware of the need for a wide theological culture that is coherent in itself and open to dialogue at the same time. Theology brings people in contact with a great tradition of thought that obviously does not exist in isolation like an erratic mass in the landscape of the spirit. The tradition can be further developed through engagement with contemporary culture; surely it need not hide its light under the bushel basket.

Thus, the reasons for this book should be clear. This introduction to moral theology is not meant to substitute for personal deepening of the subject-matter but to serve as a helpful background. Because "fundamental" moral theology provides the theoretical underpinning to the issues in "special" moral theology, the emphasis here is on foundational questions. Of course, the discussion occasionally touches on themes of special moral theology, but only to exemplify basic theoretical insights; one would need an entire life to exhaust the entire field of moral theology—a task that, given the time constraints, cannot be tackled by one thinker alone.

Nonetheless, one can find a positive aspect in this predicament in that the concentration on crucial points will at least help the reader gain a clearer orientation. The reader will be given only hints for the solution of specific issues so that she or he can deal personally with the study of more general treatises of moral theology or with detailed monographic studies. The necessity of a general introduction to moral theology is especially important when professors fail to accompany beginners in their study; the result is often a sense of impotence on the part of the student, accompanied by resignation and lack of interest. Thus, the reader ought not expect more than an introduction to moral theology.

CHAPTER ONE

CATHOLIC MORAL THEOLOGY: ITS FORM AND CHALLENGES

The Cultural Context

Catholic moral theology has always been a child of its time, and this situation holds true for the present as well. One could compare it to a seismograph of the ever-changing *Zeitgeist,* trying to reckon and deal with the many problems that affect people's lives. It would not be an exaggeration to say that moral theology must bear the first impact of new issues; our contemporaries expect from the moral theologian an answer to a profound and acute question: How is it possible to translate Christian faith into moral action in a secularized and pluralistic world, without being intellectually dishonest?

Clearly, moral theology faces a very challenging agenda—which raises another question: What form (*Gestalt*) should moral theology have, and how does this form relate to the challenges the discipline faces? Some suggestions are needed to find an orientation without losing it in a tangle of issues and approaches. No other theological discipline requires such a demanding synthesis of human sensitivity and culture.

Moral theologians work within a long tradition, yet they also work at a specific time in that tradition. On one hand, they must keep a healthy distance from the object of their reflection so they do not force themselves on their interlocutors; on the other hand, they cannot avoid personal engagement. Moral theology inevitably contains a biographical element that reflects the personality of theologians and their particular life story; through this element, moral theologians convey their proximity to life. Moral theology is anything but a

1

game of marbles played from a position of neutrality; it is a thinking exercise driven by existence itself.

Clearly, then, moral theology as a science is always relative to prescientific insight and experience. In fact, the experience of being summoned by a moral claim is common to everyone. We spontaneously rely on moral insights; we also discover in ourselves a capacity to judge, what we call *conscience*—whose dictum, following us like a shadow, cannot be dodged. The moral claim is absolute and without exceptions. It does not warrant any softening: Always and everywhere, it confronts us with the call of duty. Yet what kind of claim does morality express, and what exactly is the object of a moral demand?

First and foremost, morality concerns the reality of our being good; in this sense, any good action represents a derivative dimension, the expression of a more fundamental condition. By referring to this condition, we designate a category of our being human, a dimension of the *humanum* that is absolutely primordial. As such, it cannot be investigated further: It is simply evident, for everyone knows intuitively what it means.

Nevertheless, questions remain. These questions cluster around the content of that which we designate as morally good. What is a moral truth, and how does it distinguish itself from other kinds of truths—such as empirical, philosophical, or theological truths? A few indications might suffice. Moral truth exhibits a claim that challenges the person it addresses in the totality of her or his humanity; the possibility of living a generally successful and meaningful existence—that is, an existence that is humanly worthy—is at stake. Moral truth is truth pertaining to meaning (*Sinnwahrheit*), considered under the aspect of its relevance for action. At this point, we cannot fail to see the link between moral theology and anthropology. Indeed, central to moral theological thinking is the human being, her or his personal dignity, and the way this dignity manifests and attests itself in action.

As noted above, moral theology stands within a long tradition. We could think first of the great moral history of Christianity, especially in its ecclesial form. This history represents an impressive reservoir of wisdom and existential knowledge, now available to everyone, that can provide a first orientation in the variety and complexity of problems. The roots of moral theology reach beyond the Church, however. The community of believers recognizes its link with the rest of humanity. Indeed, the horizon of the spirit encompasses all peoples of good will. A progressive fusion of horizons takes place between believers and nonbelievers, originating in a universal ethical dialogue in which all peoples—irrespective of their religious tenets—participate. This fusion of horizons explains why we can understand each other and agree on the ethical evaluation of a particular issue even if we do not share the same religious convictions.

Correspondingly, people of the same faith can disagree on specific issues. The Church and moral theology have always been aware of this situation;

we ought not be surprised that the best elements of pagan philosophy found their way into Christianity—where, after a careful process of critical selection, purification, and transformation, they were eventually assimilated. This general phenomenon pertains not only to philosophical ideals but also to ethical insights, as one can see in the transformation undergone by the notion of *eudaimonia*. This concept allows Aristotle to define moral activity as the human *praxis* oriented to perfect and indestructible happiness. The importance of such a definition elevates morality beyond the fulfillment of duty.

What exactly is happiness, however? Because the Christian instinctively resists identifying happiness with the fulfillment of all unpurified desires and the maximization of corporeal, spiritual, or interpersonal well-being, a process of reconceptualization is needed. The Christian is not a hedonist: Her or his definition of a successful life rests on a self-understanding defined by the presence of God.

The Place of Moral Theology within the Whole of Theology

Moral theologians understand their discipline as a theological science that they pursue while standing at the center of theological reflection. Moral theology is anything but a pagan ethics with a Christian blessing; its continuity with the rest of theology should not be broken. For this reason, the interdisciplinary dialogue with each subspecialty of the theological canon remains an epistemological necessity. In this effort, the perspective of a theological anthropology will lead the way, in each case opening up the horizon of the problem. The points of contact between moral theology and the rest of theology will become evident in the following reflections.

First, moral theologians must engage in continuous discussion with their colleagues in fundamental theology. The former must know how faith can be justified in a secularized environment and rely on models of the theology of revelation elaborated by the latter; the moral theologian will justify moral claims by reference to the will of God, who has been definitively revealed in Jesus Christ.

The doctrine of God is also important for moral theologians. In fact, how should we think of God in a time of open or unspoken atheism? How is it possible to speak without misunderstandings of God as the supreme legislator? Finally, how should we reconcile the eternity of God with our temporality, and in what sense is the promise of eternal life relevant for today's action in this world?

To frame these questions already implies widening the outlook to include other theological treatises. The God of the Christian is the God of Jesus Christ. This assertion entails a recognition that there can be no moral theological reflection without explicit relation to Christology: Jesus Christ makes possible our access to the Father, so that in the Christ-event God reveals God's self to humankind. Christology must be understood as a continuous process of interpretation by the Christian community; therefore, moral theologians bring into their reflection the ecclesiastical dimension of moral knowledge and action. The Church represents a special hermeneutical context not only because it witnesses the person's conversion and sustains her or his life as an imitation of Christ; the Church is also the community that continuously rethinks the meaning of the Christian good news in relation to the challenges of the times.

Moreover, the theology of grace has to be taken into account. The moral life of the Christian directly flows from her or his being; the imperative dimension, what one *ought* to do, is grounded in the indicative—what one *is*. The reflection on being Christian developed by the systematic theologian is of great interest for moral theology; the moral theologian must rely on an understanding of grace and justification of the sinner to establish a connection with moral *praxis*. Ultimately, our action in the world is grounded in God's action toward us.

Finally, moral theology must be constantly nourished by the exegesis of both the Old and New Testament because the Scriptures represent the first sedimentation of tradition.

These brief reflections provide an account of the place of moral theology within theology as a whole. Still to be considered is where moral theology fits in the history of the Church—a history that cannot be separated from the history of the Spirit (*Geistesgeschichte*) as such. Indeed, the history of theology—particularly the history of moral theology that so closely reflects the problems of people across different generations—and the history of the Spirit are in continuous relation to one another. In this context, the Second Vatican Council has been of particular importance for moral theology. Yet we need to consider more than a purely historical outlook at the event itself. We must examine postconciliar attempts to unpack in a more systematic fashion the impulses and suggestions of what has undoubtedly been an outpouring of the Spirit.

The Second Vatican Council: A Turning Point and a Promise

The Second Vatican Council was not meant to be the council of moral theology; instead, the self-understanding and identity of the Church were in the forefront. Undeniably, however, moral theological problems were not purely secondary. In fact , the Second Vatican Council inaugurated a new era in moral theology whose long period of preparation is still to be presented.

The council's decree on the freedom of religion, *Dignitatis Humanae,* is classically referred to as a turning point; one might also speak—using the term of modern epistemology—of a "paradigm shift." The newness of the approach consists in recognizing that the reference point for moral decisions is the person's right to choose according to her or his own conscience rather than an abstract right of truth. Of course, this shift does not entail a free pass to arbitrariness. The decree underlines the fact that the person discovers in her or his conscience the immutable principles of moral order of which she or he cannot dispose and that there remains a duty to form the conscience. Thus, the document is even more significant because it finally brings closure to an era defined by the confrontation with the French Revolution, the secular state, and the modern movement for human rights. During this period, the Church gradually has come to terms with the understanding that its interests could be positively maintained by a constitutional state. By the same token, a new mindset takes shape, and personalistic categories gradually find their way into Church documents. The dignity of the person now occupies a central position; defending this dignity is the task of moral truth.

This new personalistic approach can be detected at different levels, particularly where the council talks about the Christian's call to salvation and God's original plan with humankind. The decree on priestly formation, *Optatam Totius* (16,1) sets the pace for the reflection of moral theology, bringing to an end a long, painful, and intricate history. According to this document, moral theology must find nourishment in the Sacred Scriptures. The necessity of a renewed theological agenda took shape through critical dialogue with the natural law tradition of the manuals. The moral life of the Christian should not be conceived any longer as the fulfillment of an impersonal order of natural law but as the response to a call coming from the historical person of Jesus Christ. Thus, the biblical theme of the "imitation of Jesus" makes its appearance in a Church document and becomes the main theme of moral theology; it is rightly referred to as the methodological "structuring principle" of Christian morality. This principle is characterized by a dialogical structure that brings to bear on the moral life the wealth of meaning entailed in the Christian calling to salvation. We could speak with good reason of a Christocentric approach.

The council did not limit itself, however, to the proposal of an agenda for moral theology; it actually gave initial impulses to its concrete articulation. Important methodological implications can be drawn from the correlation of Christology and anthropology sketched out in the pastoral constitution on the Church in the contemporary world, *Gaudium et Spes* (22). Here Jesus is referred to as the perfect human who reveals humanity to humanity. The meaningfulness of this idea cannot be stressed enough because it levels a criticism against different targets: an emphasis on Christology leading moral theology to a so-called "positivistic Christonomism"; the tendency to employ Scriptural passages in moral judgments on specific issues without respecting the rules of a correct hermeneutics; and the danger of a theological approach that is bound to remain external to the reality of today's problems, thus condemning Christian faith—in spite of its claim to the contrary—to practical irrelevance. The council constantly stresses the notion that Christian morality is human morality brought to its perfection. Such a statement appears to be absolutely legitimate from a theological viewpoint, especially in light of the aforementioned correlation between Christology and anthropology. At least in principle, the pitfall of a possible humanistic misinterpretation seems incompatible with the true meaning of the statement that moral theology has the task to articulate in practice. In any case, the council provides important suggestions the meaning of which the ethical consciousness of humanity cannot ignore without substantial loss.

The pastoral constitution *Gaudium et Spes* (36) underscores the autonomy of the different areas of life. Autonomy, however, must be distinguished from autarchy so that the council's statement cannot be used to support a secularized notion of ethics; indeed, one must remember that, precisely in the same context, the text emphasizes the intrinsic relation of the world with its Creator and Redeemer. Autonomy must be conceived as a "relational" or "theonomous" autonomy. Moreover, autonomy and theonomy, rather than excluding each other, stand in a relation of reciprocity in which one conditions the other. This statement is simply good Catholic theology, grounded on the classical doctrine of the analogy of being; with it stands or falls the entire edifice of Catholic theology. Indeed, one can find in this notion a profound insight already present in Thomas Aquinas—namely, that thinking rightly about God presupposes thinking rightly about God's creation.

The council's notion of autonomy does not represent a new idea within the theological tradition. On the contrary, it recapitulates a history that found paradigmatic expression immediately before the council with the "theology of world realities." The univocal intention behind this movement is the conviction that a responsible formation of the different concrete areas of life must take into account the objective laws governing them. This theology entails that a thorough analysis of phenomena must always precede the articulation of moral claims; imperatives must conform to the reality in question if Christians are not to condemn themselves to irrelevance in the name of faith. In this context believers discover the task of articulating the tension between identity and relevance: their action *for* and *in* this world must bear the burden of that tension.

Many of the council's individual statements concerning the most different realms of life and concrete fields of application can be appreciated within this horizon of thought. These issues include the transformation of the world through work, the meaning of culture in a worldwide network of communication, the importance of marriage and family as a community of life, the realities of war and peace, the need to control weapons and create international stability, and so forth. All of these urgent themes affecting the future of humanity in a world constantly growing toward globalization receive specific attention. The council provided general guidelines for moral evaluation, yet the language it used does not immediately entail a normative tone: It leaves free space for responsible evaluation. The fundamental intention of the council's fathers was to inspire the competence of moral reason.

It becomes apparent in the teaching on conscience that the council does not intend to break the link between human autonomy and God. Again, we must refer to the pastoral constitution *Gaudium et Spes* (16), which defines conscience as the hidden center of the person—that inner sanctuary where God's plan of salvation can be discovered. Critics have pointed out that this text lacks Christological dimension. Yet the connection between the Christian economy of salvation and moral life-order stands out quite univocally: Christian moral truths acquire the status of truths of salvation. Faith in the God of Jesus Christ exhibits a specific claim—namely, to provide a comprehensive horizon of understanding within which moral life unfolds and faith's responsibility for the world translates into action. Thus, conscience stands out as the unifying bond that not only comprises all areas of life but also makes them transparent to the eternal destination of humankind. Moral theologians find in these reflections the unavoidable reference point that sets the agenda for their future work.

CHAPTER TWO

HISTORICAL RETROSPECTIVE: DEFINING MOMENTS

A council does not normally happen like a bolt out of the blue sky; it is always preceded by a history—long and full of changes—that prepares its appearance. So too for the Second Vatican Council: It tried to recognize the signs of the time and find answers to questions affecting contemporary society. Those questions were not entirely new; in fact, they had been accumulating in the course of a growing exchange between moral theology and other currents of thought. Nevertheless, the council was an unavoidable reference point for the ensuing work of moral theology, and it marked a very clear turning point in the history of the field.

Moral theology itself was a forerunner that, in spite of different crises, prepared the ground for the council. This process took place at a very different pace in many countries and cultural circles. As with other disciplines, moral theology's developments depended on alternating phases and the influence of political factors within the Church. Not surprisingly, therefore, countries whose Churches could rely on a highly developed theology at a university level came to play a significant role in preparing the intellectual and spiritual *milieu* of the council. The French- and German-speaking worlds were particularly decisive in shaping the course and the results of the council.

The Influence of the German-Speaking World

The council's assertions concerning moral theology would have been unthinkable without the influence of the type of moral theology that is associated with

Bernard Häring and his manual, *The Law of Christ*. The success of that work can be explained only when we realize that it represented a critical reaction against the Latin handbooks in vogue at the time. Häring stands in the spiritual tradition of his order's founder, St. Alphonso Liguori. Häring's teacher in Tübingen, Theodor Steinbüchel (1888–1949) also had a decisive influence on Häring's thought. Steinbüchel enriched the Scholastic philosophical tradition with elements of contemporary philosophy, Kantian criticism, existentialism, personalism, the philosophy of values, and phenomenology—making them subsequently fruitful for theology.

In the same vein, Fritz Tillmann (1874–1953) should be mentioned. Formed as an exegesis scholar in Bonn, Tillmann brought into moral theology a revival of biblical thought, countering a Manualism that was driven primarily by a natural law perspective that tended to give Scriptural arguments secondary importance. Meanwhile, other theological tendencies acquired a clear profile and left their mark on moral theology: Karl Adam and Romano Guardini, to mention just two names, assisted moral theology with their emphasis on Christology and ecclesiology, respectively.

An additional trend defining the German-speaking world was the strong awareness of the need for interdisciplinary dialogue. This need was felt particularly in relation to the challenges posed to moral theology by sociology and psychology, where the influence of Sigmund Freud and Carl Gustav Jung was perceived as threatening. Moral theologians such as Theodor Müncker (1887–1960) and Werner Schöllgen stood out in this context. In the face of the growing predominance of empirical sciences in the universities, moral theology was struggling to remain a partner to be taken seriously. To do that, it could not afford the luxury of a ghetto mentality.

The same analysis applies to the philosophical tendencies of the time: They did not just pass by Catholic moral theology without leaving their profound mark. The influence of Max Scheler, for example, is worth mentioning. His "non-formal ethics of values" seemed to offer Catholic moral theologians an ally against the formalism of Kantian criticism. Moreover, Scheler's virtue-ethics was reminiscent of the Thomistic tradition. Now it could be employed to counter the Kantian ethics of duty, without any need to justify the plausibility of such an opposition. Philosophers such as Dietrich von Hildebrand, Friedrich O. Bollnow, and Hans E. Hengstenberg became trusted partners in dialogue. The influence of Josef Pieper also is not to be forgotten; his essays on virtues, which were strictly dependent on Thomas Aquinas, became part of the classical repertoire of moral theology.

Personalistic categories found their way into moral theology through philosophers such as Martin Buber, Ferdinand Ebner (1882–1931), and Eberhard Grisebach (1880–1945). According to these thinkers, recognition of the dialogical structure of the human being provides the ground for reinterpretation of the moral claim as primordially interpersonal—that is, preceding any impersonal norm. The radicalization of this line of thought found expression in the "situation ethics" eventually condemned by Pius XII, the roots of which were also influenced by existentialism (Sören Kierkegaard, Martin Heidegger, Jean Paul Sartre). According to situation ethics, norms always have an asymptotic value: The decisive element in the moral claim is ultimately the singularity of each situation.

These cursory remarks sketch out a first line of development. The picture of the German world would be incomplete, however, without mention of another very influential tendency that grew within the neo-Thomistic movement. This line of thought is associated with Joseph Mausbach (1861–1931)—a professor in Münster, a member of the "Catholic Party of the Center" *(Zentrumpartei)*, and a delegate in the *Reichstag*. Mausbach's name is inextricably linked with attempts to reform moral theology that emerged around the turn of the twentieth century but faded away very quickly. To understand them, we must look at theological developments that occurred in the course of the nineteenth century.

The dogmatic theologian Matthias J. Scheeben (1835–1888) decisively reacted against the reduction of Catholic moral theology to the level of a minimalistic and legalistic casuistry. According to Scheeben, this trend was the main reason for moral theology's poor scientific expression; thus, it was imperative to work out a renewed doctrine of the dignity of the person in Jesus Christ. The same critical reaction against a sterile neo-Scholasticism characterized the work of Johannes S. Drey (1777–1853) and Franz X. Linsemann (b.–1898). Both were under the influence of Catholic romanticism, but German idealism also created an atmosphere that was conducive to challenging theological reflections. In any case, the time was ripe for new theological projects that tried to link dogmatics and moral theology more deeply.

Neo-Scholasticism also regained some ground during the second half of the nineteenth century. A decisive event, certainly, was Leo XIII's encyclical *Aeterni Patris* (1879), which imposed a return to the sane doctrine of St. Thomas Aquinas. The ground for the retrieval of Thomas—albeit in a Suarezian tone, as it is evident in the influential Viktor Cathrein (1845–1931)—had already been prepared in Italy by Dominican and Jesuit theologians, including (among the latter) Luigi Taparelli D'Azeglio (1793–1862).

Mausbach's contributions can be understood in this historical context. His main concern was to bring moral theology back to its theological premises; at the heart of his textbook of Catholic moral theology stands the final destination of humankind in God as ultimate end. The manual was directed not only to theology students but also to members of the laity who were interested in the subject matter. Mausbach's critical confrontation with Viktor Cathrein fundamentally revolves around the theological underpinning of the discipline. Certainly, we can find in Mausbach a structure of thought based on personalistic categories, and even an incipient historical consciousness. The result was a turning away from the objectivism and essentialism of natural law categories.

Later versions of Mausbach's textbook were edited first by Peter Tischleder and then by Gustav Ermecke. The latter expanded the theological thrust of the manual into an eminently Christological one, giving a central place to the importance of sacraments in shaping a Christian's being and action. This kind of neo-Scholasticism prepared the ground for what immediately preceded the Second Vatican Council. Therefore, neo-Scholasticism clearly is too generic a term to accurately denote the variety of positions it subsumes.

The Influence of the French-Speaking World

The French-speaking world also was of paramount importance in the spiritual and cultural preparation for the council. Different lines of thought converged to create a powerful theological impulse. Under the influence of Gustave Thils and Marie-Dominique Chenu, a "theology of world realities" and a "theology of work" took shape. Eventually these reflections found an echo in the pastoral constitution *Gaudium et Spes*. Following the increasing secularization of all areas of life, there arose the need for a closer link between moral and spiritual theology; from this perspective, Dominican theologian Yves Congar made a decisive contribution to the development of a spirituality of the laity, and Gontran-Reginald Garrigou-Lagrange attempted to create a link between Thomistic systematic theology and mysticism, between theological virtues and the moral life. The scholars of Le Salchoir, including Antonin Gilbert Sertillanges (1863–1948), brought into moral theology a new kind of Thomism while seeking a dialogue with contemporary philosophy, in particular with existentialism. In the same context, a revival of Thomistic virtue ethics occurred as a result of renewed interest in the problem of moral action. The traditional teaching on conscience was retrieved in connection with the intellectual virtue of prudence (Th. Deman). Finally, the study of Thomas made it possible to rediscover the importance of *epikeia*; whereas its traditional function was to address the limits of the law and the conditions for its improvement, its meaning was now expanded to identify the virtue of the adult Christian.

The philosophical *renaissance* of the time was associated with the work of Catholic philosopher Jacques Maritain. Maritain's theoretical agenda of a *humanisme intègrale*, as well as his prophetic commitment to human rights, had a profound effect not only on moral theology but also on the official magisterium of John XXIII and Paul VI in particular. According to Maritain, Christianity brings to perfection all human dimensions. The specifically Christian element becomes accessible through the horizon of meaning opened up by faith and provides the key to understand the natural moral law binding all human beings, independent of their religion. The theorem of the *option fondamentale*, which played such a significant role in the subsequent development of moral theology, was brought into the discussion by this representative of French cultural life.

In addition to the Thomist renaissance, important contributions to moral theology came from the so-called *Nouvelle Thèologie*. After Pierre Rousselot (1878–1915) came Henri de Lubac, who brought forth a theological anthropology that was oriented to the history of salvation (particularly in his works *Surnaturel* and *Histoire et Esprit*). The result was a reinterpretation of the "nature/supernature" distinction in light of the concrete historical order. The contribution of de Lubac consists in showing how the history of salvation is concretely mediated through the history of the spirit; consequently, theology is recast as a self-interpretation of the believer, drawing from fundamental insights of theological anthropology. The theoretical links of this perspective with what would become the transcendental theology of Karl Rahner are evident.

Finally, the French world greatly contributed to moral theology with important historical research, including Odon Lottin's *Problèmes de Psychologie et de Morale aux XII.e et XIII.e siEnclès* (1942) and Thèodore Deman's *Aux origines de la Thèologie Morale* (1951).

Currents of Thought and Milestones of Modernity

Although it is necessary to appreciate neo-Scholasticism as a broad phenomenon, one could say that the efforts to renew moral theology in the twentieth century were driven by a critical reaction against neo-Scholasticism. Although neo-Scholasticism comprises different tendencies, it eventually came to represent the authoritative instrument of Church politics in the struggle against modernism. Yet it is also important to understand and appreciate the contribution of neo-Scholasticism as a defense mechanism against various currents of thought.

Neo-Scholasticism took a critical stand toward the secular ethos of the Enlightenment and its notion of happiness, although elements of the Enlightenment project—such as the systematic approach and the mathematical method (*mos geometricus*)—left their mark on neo-Scholasticism. The scientific ideal was deductive; it was based on the notion of a first principle from which all the elements of a discipline could be subsequently derived. The system thus established was valid as long as it was free from contradiction and was internally coherent. Because mathematics served as the model of an ideal science, moral principles had to be self-evident like mathematical axioms.

Another important function of neo-Scholasticism was to provide a critical stance toward the historicism and relativism of the time. Not surprisingly, therefore, moral theology put great emphasis on the immutability of the highest moral principles to secure the objectivity of moral knowledge and action. As a result, the meaning of historical changes was reduced to the variation of concrete situations that could be controlled through a strategy of casuistic application.

Finally, we cannot forget the dominant biological positivism and materialism of the time, to which moral theology reacted with an emphasis on a purely metaphysical understanding of human nature. The notion of an absolute metaphysical human nature that was the immediate and universal rule of morality (*natura metaphysica et absoluta hominis tamquam regula proxima et homogenea moralitatis*) was formulated by Gabriel Vasquez (1551–1604); this concept served as an immutable moral criterion and thus became the pillar of neo-Scholastic natural law doctrine.

In short, the cultural climate of the second half of the nineteenth century forced Catholic moral theology into a defensive attitude, resulting in the creation of a bulwark mentality. In this context, the reassuring return to Thomas Aquinas can be understood as a way to keep the system of moral theology under theoretical control. Unfortunately, this return to Thomism occurred at the price of a more serious and open scientific confrontation with the surrounding cultural environment. Catholic theology remained for a long time apologetic and completely controlled by the Church authority—particularly after the First Vatican Council. Nevertheless, sweeping generalizations are inappropriate. Indeed, one can find, as in the school of Louvain, attempts to integrate Kantian criticism into genuinely Thomistic categories (Cardinal D. Mercier, 1851–1926, and J. Maréchal, 1878–1944). The influence of Karl Rahner's transcendental theology on moral theology would be unthinkable without reference to these earlier systematic endeavors.

Associating neo-Scholastic moral theology only with a rigid, essentialistic, and ahistorical system of natural law, or with casuistry, would be unfair. This type of theology reflected, in part, a virtue ethics of genuine Thomistic ascendency (B. H. Merkelbach, 1871–1942, and A. Lehmkuhl, 1834–1918). In any case, the historical influence of the Enlightenment cannot be denied, particularly in the concern for the formation of a moral personality. Notwithstanding the importance of more foundational issues, moral theology took its pedagogical function no less seriously.

Precisely in this perspective, it becomes necessary to rehabilitate the role played by casuistry. Its outgrowth certainly damaged the scientific reputation of moral theology; on the other hand, one should not overlook the fact that, especially after the renewal of the sacrament of confession at the Council of Trent, moral theology was immediately put to the service of the clergy's practical formation. The handbooks of confession of the Irish-Scottish monks served as a model for case-oriented manuals; they provided priests in pastoral care with ready-made answers to different life problems. As a consequence, the speculative thrust of moral theology receded into the background, and the theological underpinning of ethical arguments turned increasingly formal. At the same time, some themes that originally were integral to moral theological reflection fell under the aegis of dogmatic theology—a shift that (in spite of some practical benefits) harmed moral theology in the long run. Our discipline gained a sense of concreteness—but not without lowering the speculative dimension and argumentative consistency. Ultimately, the price was too high: Confronted with the scientific rigor of dominant culture, moral theology was found wanting and thus lost its credibility as a science.

The same circumspection should be applied to the reforming efforts of Alphonso Liguori, the patron of moral theology and a saint of the Enlightenment. His most significant contribution concerned the realm of so-called moral systems; their function was to help in the solution of emerging doubts of conscience and to facilitate practical certitude regarding the morality of concrete decisions. Alphonso tried to mediate between two diametrically opposed approaches: the system known as "probabilism," on one hand, and "tutiorism" on the other. With the introduction of a third system—"equiprobabilism"—between these two, he thought he could avoid their eventual extremes—namely, laxism and rigorism (Jansenism). According to the theory of equiprobabilism, the agent's conscience can feel free from a certain precept when the reasons favoring the existence of a duty and those against it are perfectly balanced. The solution ultimately relies upon the correct use of reason; equiprobabilism is meant to make possible a decision that is intellectually sound and responsibly honest.

We are dealing here with a typically modern problematic that was prominent since the time of Nominalism. We thereby lose the link with a grounding cosmic context; the significance of personal responsibility for a conscious decision comes to the fore, together with a new emphasis on concrete and empirical dimensions of reality. Moral theology did not remain completely unaffected by this cultural shift, even if regarding Nominalism as a decline from the heights of Thomistic speculation would be an oversimplification. Indeed, Nominalism heralds most of modernity's questions and characteristics—among them, the passion for systematic thinking and the interest in epistemology.

CHAPTER THREE

THE DECISIVE FACTOR: TOWARD A THEOLOGY OF CONSCIENCE

The Second Vatican Council: Teaching and History

The Second Vatican Council tried to interpret the signs of the times and find answers to questions at the heart of contemporary humanity. Among them, the question of God occupies a very important place. How is it possible to talk responsibly and convincingly about God in a secularized, self-sufficient, and even trivialized world? What does it mean that God determines all reality and—as in moral theology—is predicated as the ultimate ontological ground (*Seinsgrund*) of moral obligation?

The language of official Church teaching constantly refers to the idea of God's plan with humanity. How should we understand this language in relation to the moral dimension? If ethical imperatives are evident in themselves and—precisely on account of this self-evidence—obligatory, why do we need any reference whatsoever to God as Creator of all things or to God as the Lord of history? Moreover, even if we assume that God exists, what does the reference to God as the highest legislator mean? In what sense should we think of ethical imperatives as God's claims to humanity, without being accused of intellectual dishonesty? Does not such a language invalidate the significance of any theoretical effort in the realm of morality and simply delegate to a transcendent authority the burden of responsibility for our own actions? Isn't a flight from the difficult task of thinking a flight from subjectivity itself?

All of these questions ought to be taken seriously because they convey so much of our contemporary self-understanding. Moral theologians are obligated to take them into account and address them in their argumentation; otherwise, they end up speaking in a vacuum and losing the interlocutor of their reflections. Moreover, they run the risk of completely missing reality and ultimately becoming irrelevant.

Contemporary sensibility regards the appeal to conscience as extremely important; conscience stands for the person's dignity and for individual responsibility in moral life. This notion is particularly important in the context of a pluralistic and tolerant society that has made the duty to actively respect the other's conscience—including in cases of disagreement—a central component of its political program. The widespread conviction that everyone knows what conscience is may explain why the Second Vatican Council decided to face the issue with an authoritative pronouncement in which it directly linked morality to the question of God—thus reviving biblical and patristic modes of thinking.

For the council's Fathers, conscience identifies a particular hermeneutic situation in which God discloses God's plan to a person; therefore, it is the most interior sanctuary and the central dimension of a person's life that bears responsibility for all of her or his moral decisions. Such a notion of conscience presupposes that the person is capable of a lived and direct consciousness of God—a kind of spiritual intuition (*geistige Anschauung*) surpassing any form of empirical experience (*empirische Anschauung*). This intuition allows the person to grasp with infallible certitude the highest moral principles of which she or he cannot dispose: indeed, she or he must recognize them as posited by God.

The course set by the council did not come about by chance; it was the result of a theological groundwork toward a more biblically oriented moral theology. The study of Scripture reveals that the concept of conscience (*syneidesis*) emerges first in "Wisdom literature" and was borrowed from Hellenistic thinking. One already encounters in the first writings of the Old Testament the word "heart" (*leb*) to designate the most interior dimension of the devout Israelite who is confronted with the keen judgment of God over her or his actions. God scrutinizes the heart and the inmost being of the person so that nothing escapes God's sight, all the thoughts and wishes of a person, all of her or his aspirations, are before God's eyes. This conception points to what is distinctive about human beings: Only the awareness of God's judgment can grant ultimate freedom from the judgment of others. The very dignity of the person consists in being judged by God only and in living in harmony with her or his own conscience. Clearly, this conception represents a landmark in the history of the human spirit, the depth and importance of which cannot be stressed enough.

The New Testament makes use of the Hellenistic language in talking about conscience (*syneidesis*), yet it also changes that language in many ways. On one hand, conscience refers to the power of moral judgment with which every person, whether believer or nonbeliever, is endowed (Rom 2:14); together with that connotation, the term takes up an additional meaning—that of an internal tribunal or a witness that, explicitly or implicitly, signifies a direct relationship to God.

The patristic literature retrieves the biblical perspective, but the philosophical elements of the Stoa and neo-Platonism also enrich the picture, making possible a first theological systematization. Augustine is particularly important for the Western tradition of thought. He associated for the first time the reality of conscience with the image of the voice of God. To understand this image, one must view it not as an infallible oracle but, against the backdrop of the "theory of illumination," as a neo-Platonic theory that Augustine reinterpreted according to his theology of creation and his epistemology. It is perfectly clear, then, why conscience is defined as *sedes Dei*—that is, the privileged place in the person where God dwells.

This mystical element got lost, however, during the ensuing history of theology, making room for an increasing intellectualization and moralization of the process of moral knowledge. Thomas Aquinas can be considered the classical representative of this evolution; conscience plays a minor role in his thought, in favor of practical reason (which occupies the central position). In any case, Thomas elaborated a distinction that will become very important for the ensuing tradition: the distinction between *synderesis* and *conscientia in situatione,* or conscience considered from the point of view of its relation to a specific situation rather than in itself (synderesis). The former denotes the habitual knowledge of first and unchangeable moral principles; this knowledge is infallible, and it does not get lost even after original sin. The *conscientia in situatione*, on the other hand, translates the first principles into concrete situations and bridges the gap between the two by means of a "quasi-syllogism." At this level, errors may emerge in the form of mistaken conclusions or of incorrect situational analyses.

Conscience mediates between God and the person in the same way (to cite the metaphor Thomas Aquinas draws from the feudal system of his time) the vassal mediates to citizens the will of the emperor. As citizens can come to know the will of the emperor only through their vassal, so the person can learn the will of God only through her or his conscience. When conscience errs without its fault, the person acts without fault: The wrong conscience does not bind *per se* but only *per accidens*. Clearly relying on the argument of Thomas Aquinas, contemporary moral theology states that an invincibly erroneous conscience binds to its action and makes it good, in spite of the objective error it brings about.

Modern Challenges

During the ensuing period, new problems emerged and new cultural challenges had to be confronted. Within the context of the modern administrative state, human law became increasingly complex in every realm. Moral theology did not remain untouched by this development; it had to take on the task of providing certainty of decision in a world that was becoming more and more complicated. The clergy in pastoral care was particularly touched by this necessity: The pastor had to be able to take away or, at least, to ease the burden of decisions put on the shoulders of his flock.

Moral systems were meant to provide some help in this situation. Their function was not to solve a doubt of conscience theoretically; in this sense, they did not compete with the normative reflection that remained the proper task of scientific moral theology. Moral systems served a more humble purpose: to provide the person in doubt with a subjective, purely practical, certainty that would account for a responsible decision; this purpose was particularly urgent for situations requiring an immediate decision that could not be postponed.

The word "system" requires some clarification, however, because it represents a typical product of the culture of nominalism and modernity. The system's goal is to bring an initial order into a reality that is still out of control, thereby providing a first orientation. A system is an artificial construction of the mind that establishes a coherence among individual truths. Against this background, it is easy to understand the characteristics of each moral system. For example, "probabilism" goes back to Bartholomew of Medina (1577), though it was made popular by the Jesuits a century later. Its central thesis can be stated as follows: When there is a nonsolvable doubt about the validity, meaning, or applicability of a law to a particular situation, one may feel free from it, provided there is at least a probable opinion supporting such a position. In this case, one may apply the axiom that to act on the basis of a probable opinion is to act prudently *(qui probabiliter agit, prudenter agit)*.

Because of its similarity to the modern turn to the subject and to freedom, probabilism was considered similar to "laxism." This objection was leveled against probabilism by its declared opponents, who upheld the system known as "tutiorism" and were spiritually very close to the rigoristic theology of Jansenism. According to the latter, one has the duty to follow the most certain opinion in all circumstances. Mediating systems, such as "probabiliorism" and equiprobabilism (Alphonso Liguori), sought to find a middle ground between these extremes. Probabilism, however, never claimed to be applicable in all circumstances. In fact, it recognized its limits when established rights needed to be protected or when actions that were legally obligatory had to be secured; in these cases, one had to proceed according to tutiorism.

The claim of moral systems was simply to provide help in the decision-making process without pretending to question the objectivity of moral norms. In this sense, moral systems differ from the so-called reflex principles, which provide first orientations that are already defined by a precise moral content. To cite only a few classical examples, consider the following principles: *in dubio pro reo* (in case of a doubt, one has to grant the accused person a presumption of innocence); *nemo malus nisi probetur* (nobody is bad until the opposite is proven); *melior est conditio possidentis* (in case of a doubt concerning the ownership of a certain good, it can be presumed that the current owner is indeed the person entitled to that good); *in dubio standum est pro validitate actus* (when there is a doubt about the validity of a certain act—for example, the celebration of a sacrament—it is better to presume in favor of the validity than against it).

The problematic of conscience is a typically modern one. This notion is particularly clear in Immanuel Kant's distinction between conscience and moral judgment. According to Kant, conscience is infallible, so speaking of an "erroneous conscience" would be nonsense. One must remember, however, that Kant's understanding of conscience has changed because of his epistemological premises; the break with the Scholastic tradition is complete. Conscience appears as the internal tribunal, as God's presence in the person testifying whether she or he acted in accordance with the universal law—namely, according to duty—or as a victim of her or his own inclinations. According to this notion, conscience (*Gewissen*) reduces to a subjective state of mind (*Befindlichkeit*) that bespeaks a particular consciousness (*Bewusstsein*); as such, it is infallible for it accounts only for the goodness or badness of the motivation. The Weberian notion of an "ethics of intention" (*Gesinnungsethik*) primarily refers to this understanding of conscience. Moral judgment, on the other hand, must be distinguished from conscience: Moral judgment is subject to the possibility of mistakes because it inevitably deals with empirical contents, operating in the realm of contingent facts with all their relativity.

The Kantian understanding of conscience as an appeal to the goodness of intentions plays a major role in contemporary public awareness. Unfortunately, failure to measure the weight of the Kantian premises opens the doors to moral subjectivism. Once again, this issue provides an opportunity to remind moral theologians of their responsibility for the philosophical premises they use. It is not enough to feel comfortable within the Scholastic or neo-Scholastic tradition; a connection with contemporary philosophical tendencies must be established without sacrificing one's own intellectual identity. The teaching on conscience can be taken as paradigmatic of this need.

The Importance of Conscience Formation

Church teaching underlines the importance of conscience formation, which in itself is a lifelong effort. Of course, it is always necessary to refer to moral authorities; yet it is easy to remain prisoners of prejudices that have progressively built up in the course of our lives. We may try to free ourselves from such prejudices, yet we remain victims of stereotypes and false arguments that we have not outgrown. Perhaps they belong to a previous level of development and, therefore, cannot be reconciled with the personality of a mature Christian.

Moral theology must enter into dialogue with different versions of modern psychology; authors such as Jean Piaget and Lawrence Kohlberg, among others, bring into play some perspectives that the traditional handbooks of moral theology did not sufficiently address—for example, the importance of emotional stability for a mature and adult conscience that must be built on confidence and trust in the persons forming the first web of relations. Also worthy of interest is the analysis of different phases of development in life toward an autonomous conscience: From the first level of pre-conventional morality, the person passes through conventional and post-conventional morality that makes her or him capable of acting in a morally responsible fashion.

Moral theologians can learn a great deal from discussions of more specialized psychological issues as well as their conclusions; in particular, they need to understand that moral action is as much an actualization of the person as it is of the norm. Actions must flow from a free insight into the good; otherwise, they give rise to the suspicion that the conscience is only superficially formed. This factor is particularly important with regard to decisions that are meant to last forever—for instance, the nonrevocable choice of a particular vocation. These decisions cannot be compromised in their spontaneity by the tyranny of the superego; what is at stake here is the final happiness of a person. The formation of conscience bears the first responsibility in bringing about this final goal.

The Christian must be able to link faith and action within the context of a pluralistic society. The intellectual challenge entailed in this task may be very difficult for the individual person. Society does not release the individual from the burden of a decision; it operates within a spectrum defined by the extremes of tolerance, on one hand, and indifference, on the other. Christians should neither fear this situation nor expect much from it. Instead, they should strive for the formation of self-understanding and morally mature personalities. A purely legalistic conscience that concentrates on the fulfillment of norms cannot suffice. Indeed, a notion of morality defined by the pure observance of preformulated norms would entirely miss the present challenge. Such a paradigm is too short-sighted; it cannot possibly grasp the fullness of reality, with all its surprises. On the contrary, the individual should become able to recognize the meaning of a norm. What is needed is intelligent obedience and the gift of discernment.

Because the risk of self-deception is always lurking, conscience formation should especially strive toward truthfulness. The tradition of moral theology presents the notion of a "tender conscience." This tender conscience is a kind of moral instinct in a person: the ability to recognize in advance the presence of danger and avoid it. Prudence is also a component of a tender conscience; the prudent person knows spontaneously how much she or he can take and where the limits of her or his strength are. This situation holds true in relation to the immediate environment surrounding the person, but it also extends to a broader realm to include the shaping of the political and social life. The tender conscience recognizes the signs of the time; it possesses the competence to identify situations of moral emergency and bear the testimony of personal involvement. Finally, it has the courage of a prophetic conscientious objection—even to the gift of our lives. Our pluralistic society openly shows the tendency to level everything; therefore, relying on the testimony of the creative outsider who follows her or his conscience with integrity is all the more important.

Contemporary society exercises great pressure on its citizens, including Christians. They cannot withdraw to save their souls and leave to others the responsibility of action. Indeed, responsibility for the world means responsibility for the active shaping of reality—particularly political and social reality. In speaking of freedom of religion, the Second Vatican Council says that one comes to faith only through a free decision of conscience. Christians must become advocates of freedom of religion; otherwise, they deny the very ground upon which they stand.

The democratic constitutional state is favorably disposed to this ideal because it rests on the presupposition that citizens have already accepted the state in their conscience and support its constitution and system of laws. Correspondingly, the state respects—at least in principle—the conscience of its citizens; it does not require obedience, like the absolute state, but cooperation and readiness to partake in the construction of the common good, even when this means going beyond the letter of the law. The formation of an adult conscience must entail this attitude. Indeed, only under this presupposition will it be possible to tolerate specific instances of conscientious objection without jeopardizing the legal system. Freedom of conscience cannot possibly represent a warrant to arbitrariness.

CHAPTER FOUR

THE MEDIATION OF FAITH AND MORAL REASON

Freedom Oriented to Reason

The ultimate goal of moral instruction is to form an adult conscience. The self-consciousness of modern humanity clearly bears the marks of the Enlightenment. The ideal of our "enlightened" contemporaries is to make use of their own reason without relying on a heteronomous authority. The most appropriate word to convey the spirit of our time is *autonomy;* moral life is a function of personal self-realization—another key concept that does not necessarily entail a negative connotation as long as it rules out arbitrariness and hedonism. The notion of "self-realization" represents a reaction against obedience to moral norms that curtail the person and dilutes her or his ideals of success into the sadness of resignation; it is a reaction against a morality that takes away from people the chance of a full, happy, and meaningful life. The great sensitivity to this danger has led moral theology to put at the center of its reflection the reality of the person with her or his indestructible dignity and her or his right to happiness and fulfillment.

There also emerges an ethos oriented to a more concrete understanding of moral problems (*Ethos der Sachlichkeit*). The notion of a reality-oriented ethic bespeaks a mentality that is more congruent with a society driven largely by a scientific model, even in its understanding of morality itself. According to this mentality, moral claims must be rationally argued and grounded in the nature of things; they should not exert any constraint on freedom. The more rational and open to argumentation a moral claim is, the more it can address the person in a manner that is respectful of her or his freedom. The only constraint in morality should be the power of the arguments that are used to persuade.

Moral theology is undertaken within a larger theological spectrum: It is a genuinely theological science whose criteria are used by all other theological disciplines. Yet it distinguishes itself in the canon of theological disciplines by playing a mediating function between theology and all other sciences that have the reality of the human being as their object of inquiry. Its internal tension, therefore, is greater. On one hand, moral theology understands itself to be without question a "science of faith" (*Glaubenswissenschaft*); on the other hand, it is no less a "worldly science" (*Weltwissenschaft*), in the sense of relating to the concrete world.

Such a demanding methodological program requires us to pass through a range of problems. Moral theologians must be not only good theologians but also thoroughly familiar with the disciplines that are relevant in the formulation of different issues within their own field of expertise. Moral theology is an open and dynamic system; moral theologians must pursue such openness by seeking to understand others and avoiding any seclusion into a cultural ghetto. Their reflection develops on the presupposition that there is no exclusive Christian ethos. Christian morality is human morality brought to its perfection—so it can be understood by all people of good will. Finally, even the Church magisterium directs itself to all people of good will when it speaks on moral matters; in so doing, it presupposes the reality of universal communication.

Models of Moral Theological Thinking

In the recent past, fundamental moral theology has paid particular attention to the fact that the Church cannot become a cultural and social outsider; it must remain a sign of unity among people, not a sect. This idea, however, translates into different theological models that still wield great influence. These models can be reduced schematically to two paradigmatic and reciprocally challenging approaches. Both models—one known as "autonomous morality in a context of faith" and the other as "ethics of faith"—try to raise equally important concerns, though from different perspectives. For this reason, the impression, ultimately, is of a pseudo-conflict between the two positions.

The first model, "autonomous morality in a context of faith" (*Autonome Moral im Kontext des Glaubens*), takes as its starting point the autonomy of human realities stressed by the pastoral constitution *Gaudium et Spes*—even if the notion of autonomy is now opened up to include the fact of moral reason. According to this model, then, moral claims must distinguish themselves for their rational plausibility and be open to argumentation. Any impression of heteronomy cannot be reconciled with true morality because the latter is essentially based on respect for freedom.

This notion of moral autonomy does not necessarily imply that Christian revelation is irrelevant to moral knowledge and action; it only entails a critique of inadequate expectations on revelation's contribution and meaning. For instance, one cannot directly appeal to revelation to justify "categorial" action norms—that is, norms directed at concrete areas of life. Although the terminology is not completely wrong, it is nevertheless unfortunate because it spontaneously brings to mind typical categories of Kantian criticism. Given the model's general epistemological presuppositions, therefore, we must first explain how these categories can fit a different intellectual tradition, such as neo-Scholasticism.

Let us return to the central question, however. In what does the relevance of Christian revelation consist? The model of autonomous morality tries to answer this question in a variety of ways. First, because the model takes faith and revelation to pertain essentially to the sphere of motivation, the two do not seem to add new moral content to the universally valid realm of natural law. The immediate consequence is that there can be no "specifically" Christian ethics, and Christians cannot vindicate for themselves any particular position with respect to the knowledge of moral norms. From the point of view of content, natural moral law and *lex Christi* ultimately overlap. One could say that believers and nonbelievers act in the same way but differ in their motivations.

A second way in which the model of autonomous morality answers the question of the significance of Christian revelation is to retrieve Jacques Maritain's notion of a "Christian horizon of meaning." Natural law binds all persons to the same moral tenets, yet it receives through the notion of a Christian horizon of meaning something like a new hermeneutic key. This concept implies certain consequences in relation to the content of natural law as well because normative contents are now being recast through an act of interpretation. According to Alfons Auer, faith exercises a threefold function in relation to moral reason: It criticizes, stimulates, and integrates the moral natural law that is logically prior to faith. Thus, the notion of a horizon of meaning emphasizes a dialectic effectual history (*eine dialektische Wirkungsgeschichte*) between faith and reason that can be reduced to the idea of a maieutic function of faith toward reason.

The model known as "ethics of faith" (*Glaubensethik*) raises critical reservations against the idea of an autonomous morality. Fearing an increasing secularization of ethics, it foresees the notion of autonomy quickly turned into autonomism, with the subsequent collapse of the distinction between "ethos of salvation" (*Heilsethos*) and "world ethos" (*Weltethos*). The immediate consequence is the sinking of lived moral standards and the tendency to a complete flattening of Christian morality into a secularized ethos.

Moreover, from a theological point of view the model of autonomous morality operates on an understanding of revelation that is extrinsic and essentially sanctions secular ethics with only a Christian blessing; in addition, by concentrating exclusively on normative ethics rather than on an ethics of virtue from the Thomistic model, it fails to provide an accurate account of the reality of human action. Moral action is not immediately defined by the categorial norms it is supposed to fulfill but by the goals and ideals it pursues. Normative ethics must be viewed within the framework of a virtue ethics that formulates the correlation of the theological virtues of faith, hope, and charity with the four cardinal virtues of prudence, justice, fortitude, and temperance and brings into this correlation both infused and acquired virtues.

From a critical point of view, however, because an ethics of faith is unable to show that there are formally revealed categorial action norms, it cannot dispense with the work of moral reason. As a result, the contrast between the two models ends in a stalemate. Perhaps what is really at work here is a pseudo-conflict resulting from different and (in both directions) legitimate interests. The model of an autonomous morality is concerned primarily with the problem of universal communication; it attempts to prevent Christian morality from falling into practical insignificance. On the other hand, an ethics of faith aims at recovering the public relevance of Christian identity and the "specificity" of a moral reason enlightened by faith. It regards the believer as standing in a privileged position in relation to the nonbeliever—as someone who can bring into universal moral communication an absolutely unique contribution.

Anthropological Correlates of Faith

Moral truths acquire for the believer the status of truths of salvation; the moral life of the believer derives from sanctifying grace and leads to eternal happiness. Yet how should we think about this particular status, granted that there is no formally revealed moral truth and that we must refrain from overinterpreting the meaning of Christian revelation?

The transcendental theology developed by Karl Rahner can offer an important contribution to the solution of this problem, leading to the programmatic notion of the anthropological coordinates of Christian faith. Theology can speak of God if it starts from the reality of the human being; ultimately, theology becomes possible only through the mediation of anthropology. Truths of faith generate a system of anthropological coordinates that, though not formally revealed, remains under the direct influence of faith; such a system maps out the essential elements of faith's self-understanding that, in their turn, can mold a Christian horizon of meaning. The system of anthropological coordinates represents the fruit of *ratio fide illuminata* (reason enlightened by faith) and bears witness to the fact that faith truly represents an *obsequium rationi humanae consentaneum* (a respect or submission congruent with human reason). Because faith is not incompatible with reason, any voluntaristic interpretation must be avoided; because it also transcends reason, however, it brings into the picture an additional component that needs to be thought out. The anthropological implications of faith represent open dimensions of meaning *(Sinngehalte)*. Their intellectual content must be disclosed through a continuous hermeneutic effort.

One of these implications is the indestructible dignity of the person. Because the person stands within the horizon of faith, her or his ontological ground includes a direct and lived immediacy with God. Consequently, moral norms effectively shield this new quality of the person's dignity through a process of understanding that remains historically determined. The anthropological implications of faith extend to other notions—for instance, the fundamental equality of all human beings grounded in the incarnation and the new quality of history inaugurated by the Easter event. The fact that God equals God's self to a human being in Jesus Christ constitutes the ground for the equality of human beings among themselves.

Again, the inventive power of moral reason must concretely articulate the meaning of this key concept; only under this condition can one make use of such a notion in an intellectually controllable way. This notion sketches out a general counter-program to the natural tendencies of the person, which is to set up and uphold inequalities. Certainly, it is impossible to completely get rid of inequalities; nevertheless, they must be justified without compromising the equal dignity of all persons.

Another implication of faith concerns the new quality of history inaugurated by the Easter event. Because God reveals God's self to all people in an historical event and shares with them indestructible meaning, a situation exists in which no historical event could be prevented from acquiring some dimensions of meaning. This situation applies, in particular, to the reality of death with all its temporal anticipations: Death is no longer an irrevocable catastrophe that the person has to avoid at all costs; instead, it becomes the journey into eternal life. For this reason, every situation of suffering stands within the horizon of meaning defined by the Easter event. For the believer, no situation can be completely hopeless, even when one is facing the final limit of death. The believer lives her or his existence in the anticipation of death; in so doing, the believer has already transcended it.

A final implication of faith that is reflected in the system of anthropological coordinates relates to the theology of grace. The fact that God gratuitously gives God's self over to humankind bears profound consequences for the structure and form of human relations. The latter share now in the gratuitousness of the former, so that interpersonal relations can become a symbol of God's relation to the person. Moreover, the primacy of God's love represents the ultimate perspective from which to judge and criticize every system of law; human institutions are never an end unto themselves but only a means toward something else.

Moral theology acknowledges the fact that these anthropological implications provide only a programmatic framework, a system of coordinates that must be further completed. The inventive power of moral reason is necessary to take up the data provided by the anthropological implications of faith and develop them constructively. Faith neither shelters itself from the risk of this reflection nor substitutes itself for moral reason; it inspires moral reason through its anthropological implications. Therefore, moral theology cannot be equated with a pure deductive science. Moral norms cannot be immediately derived from faith or put in direct correlation with faith; the two belong to different levels of discourse, each characterized by its own epistemic status.

This conclusion in no way diminishes the relevance of faith for morality. Morality provides protection from the danger of overinterpreting the meaning of faith assertions. The subjective principle of moral knowledge remains the *ratio fide illuminata*; the light shed by faith reflects itself in the system of coordinates that define theological anthropology.

The Biblical Argument in Moral Theology

The foregoing analysis also applies to the issue of how to deal appropriately with biblical texts of the Old and New Testament. Scripture cannot be conceived as a handbook of moral theology, nor does it present any ethical system that could provide a ready-made answer for every area of life. Scripture recounts, through a variety of literary genres, the story of the chosen people reaching its fulfillment and critical turning point in the Jesus event.

This insufficiency of Sacred Scripture is twofold, at least. We can observe, first, the lack of a formal process of ethical argumentation. The biblical authors do not develop an independent theological-moral method that would meet the criteria of today's epistemology. We should not forget that a clear methodological awareness began developing with nominalism and that theology did not eschew the challenge of continuously renewing its scientific status to remain a serious interlocutor within the scientific landscape. Indeed, it was important for theology not to be confined to a cultural ghetto; the public relevance of theology was at stake. Scripture's insufficiency does not mean, then, that ethical argumentation is completely lacking in the Sacred Scripture—only that it has a fairly limited space compared with the literary genre of *parenesis* (sometimes also referred to as *paraclesis*). Parenesis presupposes in the reader it addresses the presence of a certain moral insight; from that insight, it tries to stimulate and deepen the level of motivations by reference to God's action in Jesus Christ. In sum, exhortation already entails an underlying argumentation.

There is, however, a second and more decisive insufficiency having to do with content. The Scripture does not provide any moral theological treatise.

When it addresses specific questions, it does so with statements that are mainly intended for the particular occasion. Therefore, an intelligent moral theological hermeneutics is required to make possible the translation and application of specific biblical statements to present-day life, which is defined by very different social, cultural, and historical conditions.

The perspective of the exegesis scholar remains necessarily limited in facing this problem; the moral theologian must carry out the burden of a final interpretation. Often, all the moral theologian can do is simply convey the exhortatory thrust of certain Scripture statements, together with motivations and the reference to the charisms. Clearly the biblical authors and the communities behind them did not have any idea of today's issues. The Sacred Scripture does not offer an immediate answer to all the problems we face. It is neither a storehouse nor a quarry; for this reason, the moral theologian must develop the biblical position further with an additional hermeneutical analysis.

The concept of reason with which moral theologians operate is theologically defined through and through; a notion of reason modeled after the paradigm of an ahistoric and generic reason (*eine profillose Allerweltvernunft*) is not suitable for theology's own object. Instead, the theologian relies on a notion that can carry out the task of *intellectus fidei* (the intelligence of faith), a notion characterized by its relational autonomy—daring to think about God and penetrate God's inscrutable mystery. The same notion of God undergoes an historical process of reflection that then affects the analysis of the surrounding world-reality.

Moral reason enlightened by faith enters into both thought processes. On one hand, it participates in the formal structures of universal human reason (*allgemeine Menschheitsvernunft*); on the other, it transcends them. In this way, it becomes possible to unpack the inconceivable depth of the anthropological implications of faith and to lay them out to the nonbeliever as the best alternatives for action. The moral reason of the believer does not adapt itself uncritically to existing standards of moral insight, repeating what everybody already says. Indeed, this would be the triumph of boredom! Instead, moral reason enlightened by faith brings its constructive contribution to universal ethical dialogue by articulating to all people of good will the significance of its own presuppositions.

Rational plausibility, however unavoidable and necessary, also remains inevitably abstract. It searches for the visibility of living signs. We cannot simply hint at better alternatives; we also must concretely live them out. Only under this condition can they attract and liberate at the same time. In the end, it is impossible to live without the testimony of moral personalities characterized by spiritual and intellectual sensitivity.

CHAPTER FIVE

THE ECCLESIAL DIMENSION OF CHRISTIAN MORALITY

Existence as Communication

Human existence essentially unfolds in a communal way, and the realm of morality partakes in this dimension. Therefore, it would be a grave misunderstanding to relegate morality to the private sphere of the person and allow natural mechanisms of self-regulation and technocratic efficiency to dominate the public sphere. Indeed, moral truth demands the commitment of the entire person in all her or his dimensions and relations: the interiority of intentions no less than the exteriority of deeds.

Moral knowledge and action are inevitably shaped by particular communities; nobody lives like a windowless monad. Not surprisingly, this description holds true for people of faith as well; they live their Christian existence within the protective womb of mother Church because faith was communicated to them through community and tradition. Salvation does not suspend the natural structures of humankind; it permeates, elevates, and changes them.

In a very profound sense, human communities are communities of communication. Communication represents the primordial life-process of humankind. Because language is bound to the person's ability to speak, it also represents the primordially grounding human institution. One could say that language is like a "meta-institution": It is the condition for the very existence of every other institution. Human beings develop words, and words, in turn, become meaning-full symbols; the possibility of communication stands or falls with the univocity of their meaning.

At the same time, language remains a live reality that reflects the historical mobility of the human spirit. The progress of knowledge and thought discloses new perspectives and unknown points of view to the world, deepening and sharpening traditional insights. Language partakes in this process: New concepts are continuously created, and existing concepts acquire different meanings. Moreover, the coordination of concepts in sentences and sequences makes possible an unlimited variety of combinations.

Interpersonal communication mirrors this dimension of historical mobility. Thus, semantic and hermeneutic efforts are required for our life together to succeed without breaking apart into a series of misunderstandings; intellectual responsibility becomes an act of public solidarity whereby the complexity and conflictuality of existence is reduced to a bearable measure that makes culture possible.

The Church as Moral *Communio*

The ecclesial dimension of Christian morality fits harmoniously into this perspective. The ecclesiology of Vatican II stressed certain aspects that may have a fruitful application in moral theology. The Church stands out as the people of God in pilgrimage through time toward its final eschatological promise and fulfillment in which God will be all in all. Before taking up a juridical and institutional form (*Gestalt*), the Church is the living *communio* of the believers.

This fact has moral implications concerning, first, the process of moral knowledge. The Church is a community of memory, understanding, and interpretation in which the original encounter with Jesus the Christ lives on and remains present. Thus, with continuously renewed efforts, the Church returns to its beginnings, trying progressively to capture all the spiritual and intellectual fullness of that foundational event and to articulate its meaning in the succession of time. To be sure, the Church cannot isolate itself and must abstain from an attitude of self-sufficiency. Its mission is to face cultural movements of each era as challenges whose confrontation mobilizes its best forces and intellectual elites.

Moreover, if faith stimulates thought, the reverse—thought stimulates faith—is no less true; the Anselmian formula *fides quaerens intellectum* (faith seeking understanding) must be completed by the corresponding statement, *intellectus quaerens fidem* (understanding seeking faith). The Church can be compared to an open, dynamic system whose self-understanding benefits from the exchange with contemporary epistemology. The Church should be defined by a communal thinking effort in which all members of the community participate and share—albeit in different measure—the same responsibility. The tradition thus generated is a living reality that is open to continuous correction.

The moral tradition of Church can be analyzed in light of this perspective. This tradition assimilates insights from the outside and returns them to humankind, having read them through the filter of a Christian conception of the person. The Second Vatican Council speaks—not without historical basis—of the common spiritual treasures the Church shares with humanity at large. The Old Testament exhibits a spiritual and intellectual openness to the surrounding cultures—in particular, to the best elements of Hellenistic ethics; the idea of "osmosis" may best capture the essence of this process. The same can be said for the Judeo-Christian communities described by the Pauline and deutero-Pauline letters. This openness does not compromise the identity of the churches; the presupposition is that even outside the community of believers there are authentic moral insights. St. Paul's critique of the moral lifestyle of the pagans does not change the general validity of this point; in fact, it presupposes it.

Moral communication takes place beyond the limits of the visible and institutionally defined Church because the Church understands itself as the "agency" that paves the way and provides a forum to universal understanding. Insofar as it represents a sign of unity among peoples and a principle of universal friendship for all mankind, the Church is anything but a self-contained sect. The universality of its mission reminds the Church that it must open its knowledge and thought to the understanding of all people of good will. To be a "sign of salvation," the Church must understand itself as mission-oriented and have an attitude of invitation and openness. This attitude has nothing to do with blurring the Christian identity into a generically rational moral common sense; it means making available to everyone the implications drawn from the cognitive preeminence of faith (*Erkenntnis Vorsprung des Glaubens*) while maintaining a disposition to learn from others.

The Church as *communio* is not only a community of memory, knowledge, and thought; it is also a community of brothers and sisters who live and witness concrete solidarity. St. Augustine rightly refers to the Church as *caritas*. The importance of this insight reflects the institutional self-understanding of the Church by making clear that it transcends the hierarchical structure of a purely official Church (*Amtskirche*). Of course, one has to recognize the presence of specific and separate functions within the Church, such as a particular office (*Amt*) established by God with a magisterial function in moral matters and the authority to speak to the conscience of believers.

The Church's magisterium claims for itself the right to lay out and explain authentically the entire natural moral law and retains for itself the competence to define moral truths that are not formally revealed. It also requires from the believer an *obsequium religiosum* that is more than purely disciplinary obedience. The Church does not shy away from canonical sanctions, yet anyone who advances a claim must be sensitive to the justification grounding it. Undermining this obvious fact would imply that the Church is unfaithful to its very nature and fails in the exercise of its authority. The Church moves from the presupposition that whatever it brings forth as God's claim and plan with humankind can be evident to everyone's conscience. This premise, however, does not spare the Church the burden of argumentative openness. All the cards have to be on the table: One cannot appeal to conscience, on one hand, and on the other step over that very conscience in the name of authority by failing to take seriously its critical function.

Every believer, whether layperson or clergy, is a responsible partner of the magisterium. For this reason, nobody should fail to contribute to the development of the living moral tradition of the Church. All are invited to bring to the ecclesial dialogue their own professional and human expertise, even when they may be uncomfortable interlocutors; no morality ever sank from excessive honesty. We may need to retrieve the profound insights of Pope Paul VI's first encyclical, *Ecclesiam suam,* which emphasizes the spirit of dialogue in an almost dramatic way.

The Church is defined by a widespread moral consensus; partial dissent on particular issues should not convey the wrong impression. Indeed, the Church does not hesitate to admit that it cannot have a definitive answer to all particular moral questions and that different conclusions can follow from common principles. This notion entails an agenda of reflection that calls for the concerted effort of all the members of the Church. The main question concerns the nature and logic of the link between truths of faith and moral truths.

Moral truths cannot be directly derived from truths of faith. Even the magisterium cannot pass over their different epistemic status; it remains bound to the universal rules defining the search of truth, its privileged position notwithstanding. The tendency of the Church in this context is to show the meaningful reciprocity of faith and moral truths, to make room for justifications of convenience, and to rely heavily on them to build a secure tradition that can be trusted in cases of doubt. Thus, the claim of the magisterium is sufficiently grounded; its pronouncements can embrace the results of a long tradition of thought that prevents moral insights from getting lost in the Church.

One should not forget, however, that tradition remains a living reality that is open to continuous deepening and correction; some tiles of the mosaic may get replaced and new ones added. The magisterium is aware of that process, and it clearly recognizes the possibility of progressively sharpening its teaching while facing the challenge of new problems. What prevails, however, is a concept of historical continuity in the magisterial teaching that borders on the mechanistic. Yet why should we rule out the possibility of profound intellectual changes in history? Why do we need to think of progress in terms of linear continuity? If we take for granted that discontinuities and changes occur in the history of the spirit (*Geistesgeschichte*), why should we not admit that the same happens for the Church as well, provided it does no harm to the credibility of the magisterium and its teaching mission?

Perhaps the key to all these questions lies in the Church's conception of truth and how it defines the relationship between truth and history. Indeed, we avoid the pitfall of losing reality in either abstraction or relativistic facticity only by taking seriously the notion of historicity *(Geschichtlichkeit)*.

Historicity of Truth and Structures of Thought

Historicity of truth means recognizing the conditions for the discovery of truth and making them relevant in the elaboration of moral judgment; a keen hermeneutic awareness is thereby required. This perspective applies to the problem of dealing with the understanding of magisterial documents and to the critical question concerning the degree of authority that the Church invests in specific instances. The importance of a document normally depends on its genre, unless there is an explicit indication to the contrary. An encyclical, for example, is more important than a *motu proprio* or a pastoral instruction, not to mention speeches for particular occasions. The language also provides a key to the interpretation of a document, especially if it refers to the continuity of tradition. Yet these preliminary clarifications do not exhaust the hermeneutical problem; one must also take into account the presuppositions of magisterial teaching. What has become obvious in relation to Scripture applies even more to the problem of dealing with the texts of the magisterium: They are children of their time and carry with them the signature of their genetic context; thus, they could be further developed and, in any case, must undergo a process of interpretation.

There is an additional question, however, concerning the relationship between the form or structure of thought *(Denkform)* and its content *(Denkinhalt)*. Could a consolidated form of thought become incapable of grasping new contents and fashioning them linguistically? Doesn't the Church need to critically test its categories of thought and verify their suitability?

It is correct to underline that the magisterium of the Church does not depend on specific philosophical currents or schools of thought and that its teaching has a consistency of its own. Yet even the magisterium cannot avoid making use of philosophical arguments, the opposite impression notwithstanding. Surely it establishes a link—too quickly, some people think—between the natural moral law and the law of Christ; yet the decisive argumentation is based on the natural law. In addition, the magisterium relies on the assistance of the Holy Spirit because it operates on the presupposition of the Church's infallibility as a whole.

If the magisterium argues essentially on the basis of natural law, then, it must remain open to a process of intellectual self-revision. The Holy Spirit calls for such action to take place through the constructive criticism of people of faith; after all, they have to live with the magisterium's indications.

Something like a duty of co-responsibility, of thinking-together, should be carried out primarily by philosophy and theology not in the exclusivity of an ivory tower but in close contact with the concrete moral experience of all areas of life. In this way, a critical function keeps the theology of the magisterium in a healthy dynamism. The *sensus fidelium* (the communal understanding of all the believers) provides the magisterium with its feedback, and the Holy Spirit makes sure that the Church will not open the doors to any error in a definite way.

We could say that the *receptio* of a certain teaching by the whole people of God essentially contributes to its validity. This statement in no way entails reducing the authoritative function of the magisterium in moral matters; on the contrary, it embeds such authority within a larger framework in which the *ecclesia docens* (teaching Church) is viewed in its structural orientation to the *ecclesia discens* (learning Church). The *sensus fidei populi Dei* (sense of faith of the people of God) is the capacity of the people of God to discern the nexus between salvation and moral truth—a capacity that is constantly challenged by the experience of moral success or failure. The renewed ecclesiology of the Second Vatican Council in relation to the theology of the magisterium cannot be superseded by a hierocratic move.

The mindset (*Denkform*) of the magisterium is clearly theological, and this fact must be taken into account when the magisterium claims for itself the authentic presentation and interpretation of natural law. This act of interpretation cannot pursue a goal of its own because it must always remain transparent to the event of revelation. The binding power of magisterial prescriptions extends as far as its ability to meaningfully account for this transparency. Indeed, the function of the magisterium must be understood in the context of the unswerving faith of the ecclesial *communio* for which it provides official expression. Yet all this communication obviously occurs in reference to the liberating good news of Jesus Christ himself—which, in turn, is passed on to the whole Church through the Christological process of interpretation of the first community. The Church maintains the anthropological dimension of the salvific encounter with Jesus Christ.

The Church teaching inevitably conveys the radicalism of the evangelical good news. This radicalism represents an unmistakable element that in no way remains external to that proclamation but molds its every content through and through. The magisterium itself bespeaks such an awareness when—as in the theology of the magisterium of Paul VI—it refers to its prophetic function.

What does this choice of words mean?

First, it signifies the Church's unwavering support for the dignity of the person and for her or his inalienable human rights, especially in situations in which they are being trampled or misrepresented. The Church—the pontificate of John Paul II in particular—gives testimony to this responsibility. Yet limiting the meaning of the prophetic function of the magisterium to this element would be insufficient: Its roots go deeper, and the extension of its validity is wider.

The last reference point of magisterial pronouncements is the Sermon on the Mount, particularly the primary and secondary antitheses; the Church keeps alive the theological interest of the Sermon of the Mount and further articulates its meaning. The Church will decisively set itself in favor of a theologically responsible interiorization of morality, thus opposing any form of legalism and casuistic accentuation. God seeks the very heart of Christians, not individual deeds that are neatly defined and clearly limited but do not go beyond a purely external correctness. Above all, God seeks mercy: The anti-pharisaic thrust of Jesus' proclamation cannot be lost in the Church.

The Church works—especially through the living testimony of its saints—on the deterministic structures of reality defined by a history of conflict; through healing and reconciliation, it tries to break through these structures to provide better alternatives for moral action. In so doing, the Church relies on the fact that the power of fascination of its moral alternatives may appeal not only to believers but to all people of good will, thus introducing in the history of humankind a new potential full of promises. Finally, in Church teaching we find reference to the notion of "structures of sin" (*Sollicitudo rei socialis* 37). The Church does not give up on these structures; its moral proclamation is at once indicting protestation and reconciling testimony. Therefore, the Church clearly cannot be immediately equated to a particular moral institution; in spite of all its human frailties, it remains the signpost for a better humanity.

CHAPTER SIX

MORAL NATURAL LAW AS A BASIS
OF UNIVERSAL COMMUNICATION

The Insufficiency of Revelation

The moral instruction of the Church's magisterium is intended to address all
people of good will. It presupposes a universal capacity of moral judgment that
is grounded in the unity of humankind's moral consciousness—however frag-
mented, obscured, and dependent on so many cultural, anthropological, and
social conditions that consciousness may be. Differences aside, the moral theological tradition has always been confident in the notion of such a unity; relying on the resources of Greek philosophy, especially the Stoics, it developed
the doctrine of natural moral law. The need to develop this doctrine was
prompted by the awareness of the insufficiency of Christian revelation with regard to its content. Answers had to be found to questions that neither revelation nor Scripture had ever explicitly tackled.

Even the cultural world of biblical authors is already characterized by
this approach; there really never existed something like a pure "ethics of faith"
(*Glaubensethik*). This insight provides moral theology with enough reasons to
keep alive the notion of natural law; it also does not prevent moral theology
from developing it even further. What has been understood at different mo-
ments in history as natural law can assume very different forms. Yet the reality of varying—when not reciprocally contradicting—theories of natural law
does not immediately speak against its plausibility; at best, it stands as an in-
centive to engage in new theoretical efforts and to lay out a theory of natural
law that is consistent with today's scientific culture. Even the Scholastic tradi-

tion is capable of further development; it could be compared to an open system that not only permits but even requires a constructive dialogue with contemporary philosophical trends.

Milestones in Historical Development

Defining elements of natural law thinking can be found in the theology of the Fathers of the Church; Ambrose and Augustine, especially, offer examples of a dialogue pushed beyond the boundaries of theology into the realm of philosophy. Ambrose, for example, retrieves (through the mediation of Cicero) main elements of Stoic thinking about reality in terms of order (*Ordo-Denken*). The surrounding *cosmos* is regarded as an ordered totality in which everything receives its natural place and expresses the wisdom of the creator. Human beings participate in this order; insofar as they accept its intrinsic laws, they can be sure to act according to God's will. The dominating structure of thought is clearly cosmocentric; yet the cosmic order provides more than just a direction: It is also an active power within which humanity can feel sheltered. What is at work here is a mode of thinking in terms of harmony that cannot be mistaken for a kind of surreptitious naturalism; obligations do not immediately stem from nature but from the *logos* that inhabits nature and brings every being to its perfection.

Augustine, on the other hand, stands under the influence of Neoplatonism and is responsible for bringing the theorem of *lex aeterna* into the moral theological tradition. Natural moral law appears as a participation in God's eternal law and is revealed to humankind through inner enlightenment. One should read this notion against the general background of the Augustinian theory of illumination. The dominating mindset has clearly become anthropocentric: The person finds the truth in the interiority of her or his spirit, not in the visible world surrounding her or him. As Augustine says in the *Soliloqui*, (I, II, 7): *Noli foras ire, in te ipsum redi; in interiore homine habitat veritas* ("Do not go outward but remain in the inwardness of your being, for in the inner self dwells truth"). Moreover, the moral natural law participates in the unchangeableness of eternal law. Eventually, Augustine develops a theology of nature that fits perfectly into the theology of history of his *De civitate Dei*: Here the pure form (*Gestalt*) of natural law overlaps with the *lex civitatis Dei* (the law of the City of God)—namely, *caritas* (charity).

Neither Ambrose nor Augustine limits himself to the realm of abstract and theoretical speculation; each confronts the concrete issues of moral life. For instance, one finds in Augustine the foundation of the doctrine of the "just war," along with instructions on prayer, work, and the religious life.

The theology of the Fathers lays out the decisive foundation of Thomas Aquinas's teaching on natural law—which he, in turn, enriched with Aristotelian elements. As the outline of the *Summa Theologiae* makes clear, the Thomistic conception is thoroughly theological. Moral reason occupies center stage; the moral natural law is an *ordinatio rationis* (an ordering of reason) and *aliquid a ratione constitutum* (something constituted by reason). The analogy to human law is immediately evident: As the human legislator enacts laws for the sake of *bonum commune* (the common good), so God the Creator promulgates the *lex naturalis* (natural law) for the sake of *bonum universi* (good of the world). Natural law is an operative expression of the divine *gubernatio rerum* (governance of all things). Considered from a human point of view, the moral natural law appears as a participation of the rational creature in the eternal law. Clearly we can find here residual elements of the Augustinian conception. On account of being endowed with reason, the human being is *sibi ipsi et aliis providens* (*Summa Theol.* I-II, q. 94, a.2)—that is, the human being plays an active role in divine providence in providing for the welfare of oneself and others.

Another perspective emerging in Thomas that was significant for the ensuing moral theological tradition is the embodiment of moral reason within the realm of the *inclinationes naturales* (natural inclinations). Human beings share these inclinations with the other (subhuman) creatures, yet humans also possess inclinations that distinguish them from the rest; they include the need to survive, procreate, live in a community, find truth, and know God. Although Thomas remains vague on the details, the inventive power of moral reason clearly is given the responsibility to bring these inclinations to completion and to further specify their content.

One can easily object that what Thomas concretely means by acting according to reason could be clearly inferred from his works; we can think of his teaching on marriage and his understanding of marital union, or his position on religious tolerance. Nevertheless, his fundamental assertions have lasting meaning to which contemporary moral theology still must refer, even when it arrives at different conclusions on specific issues. Finally, Thomas remains—his genius notwithstanding—a child of his time; he did not have any notion of our contemporary problems, and he cannot provide us with answers to questions he never faced and of which he was not aware. We could think here of the modern sensitivity to the historical dimension of knowledge or the confrontation with empirical sciences.

Modernity begins for the moral theologian with the epoch of Nominalism. Here the medieval notion of order (*Order-Denken*) breaks asunder, and a turning point sets in: The link between God and the world becomes problematic; humanity feels homeless and begins to reflect on its own meaning. We often find in moral theological literature the view that Nominalism represents a fall in thinking from the height of Aquinas's speculation, the breaking down of his entire intellectual construction. This view is not only inaccurate from a historical perspective; it also originates from the desire of an unproblematic synthesis, as if going back to Thomas could provide us with such a synthesis. Certainly, the Thomistic synthesis fell into ruins, but a new life arose from it. The critical awareness of scientific and methodological questions grew, paving the way to modern systematic thinking; moreover, a culture based on the exact observation of phenomena provided a powerful impulse to interdisciplinary dialogue. The language of factual observation gained ground, thus making increasingly obvious that metaphysics cannot be developed against empirical presuppositions. In sum, what came about was a sense of healthy skepticism against philosophical claims of totality.

Moral theology has not remained untouched by this process, whose influence continues even today. For instance, moral theologians must be aware of hard scientific data before exhibiting a claim in the name of a normative human nature; otherwise, they run the risk of losing touch with reality. Furthermore, it is impossible to escape the extension of a scientific approach to all areas of life without turning morality into a purely private affair.

Ensuing eras have brought additional challenges to the problem of natural law. With late Scholasticism, expanding colonialism led to a broader understanding of the world—and with it the need to find a common platform of moral communication that could overcome differences of cultures and religions. The first notion of what became international law developed; at the same time, the idea of an international order of peace started to take shape. In this context, moral natural law meant a revindication of rights grounded in common human nature. There was also a parallel tendency to secularization whereby the notion of natural law developed according to its own dynamics, independent of any theological framework. This development represented a major step in the direction of what evolved during the Enlightenment into the notion of "rational law" (*Vernunftrecht*)—which, in turn, provided the basis for jurisprudence and the development of a legal system in which religious and confessional pre-decisions are methodically suspended in favor of the rational plausibility of arguments. This system seems to be the only way to respect the freedom of individuals within the moral community and their identity as bearers of rights.

An historical overview cannot pass over the names of Gabriel Vasquez and Francisco Suarez; both are responsible—albeit with different accents—for increasingly turning natural law into a rigid metaphysics. Whereas the former defines the essential human nature as the immediate ground of moral obligation, the latter works out a metaphysics of moral action. They share a concern, however, for the certitude of knowledge and the security of action to cut the ground away from any voluntaristic and subjectivistic tendency; the absoluteness and objectivity of moral claims are now metaphysically anchored. Manuals of moral theology were deeply influenced by this mindset; Suarez especially obstructed the passage to the thought of Thomas Aquinas. Ultimately, we could read the contemporary effort to retrieve the genuine Thomas as a reaction against the restrictions of the tradition, in particular its objectivistic and essentialistic notion of metaphysics. On the other hand, Thomas seems to pay attention to the reality of the moral agent; for this reason, he is closer to the sensibility of contemporary thought.

The current discussion on moral natural law cannot avoid paying attention to Immanuel Kant; indeed, criticism has been directed at the tradition for its dependency upon Kant—for standing in "the long shadows of Kant." At the center of Kantian thought stands the notion of moral autonomy, which—in typical Enlightenment mode—expresses itself in the self-determination of practical reason. Such a statement is far from any suspicion of autonomism or subjectivism; it must be understood in light of Kant's own epistemological agenda, with its dualistic distinction between theoretical and practical reason. Whereas the former, beginning with the realm of empirical phenomena, is unable to reach the "thing in itself," the latter has the power to grasp the moral claim in its absoluteness and universality, enabling one to act out of duty rather than inclination.

Contemporary moral theologians with an interest in Kant try to defend the traditional conception of natural law from the accusation of naturalism—that is, from falling into the so-called naturalistic fallacy of David Hume and G. E. Moore. Yet the Scholastic and neo-Scholastic traditions of moral theology never thought of a direct passage from "is" to "ought"; at most, that tradition could be accused of working with a reductive conception of being. A naturalistic fallacy always presupposes a naturalistic notion of human being. The Scholastic and neo-Scholastic traditions did not include such a premise, however. They both kept themselves far from such a reduction because their theory of natural law—its persuasiveness aside—was always based on a metaphysically grounded anthropology.

Crucial Points in the Contemporary Debate

This inevitably cursory overview sketches out, at least in general terms, the framework of contemporary discussion and foreshadows its possible outcome. The discussion on natural law of the past decades is defined primarily by a critical reaction to the tradition—which, in fairness, was richer than its reputation. Moreover, the discussion reveals a moral theology that is eager for dialogue with contemporary philosophical currents of thought; the search for a new philosophical partner is based on the conviction that the absence of a serious intellectual exchange would certainly condemn the tradition to death. Finally, the discussion on natural law is dominated by a critical attitude toward Church documents; a natural law perspective seems prevalent in those documents, even when they employ a philosophical personalism that is not always clearly defined. The following points of crystallization highlight an ongoing, polyvalent discussion.

The first point in the reflection concerns the problem of articulating the relationship between nature and person; here, moral theology brings to full expression a structure of thought *(Denkform)* that is already outlined by Church documents. The goal is to find a middle ground between the extremes of a personalism that is forgetful of nature, on one hand, and a naturalism that is inattentive to the person, on the other. Such a mediating position would not only be theoretically convincing; it would also lead to solutions that seem reconcilable with the notion of a responsible moral life. The relevance of the biological dimension is in no way suspended; it certainly provides important hints in the formulation of moral judgment. Thus, the impression of an anthropological dualism is excluded from the outset. Of course, the biological nature provides essential elements that must be thought out. Recognition of its relevance for ethics does not mean that nature is immediately normative; to assume that would entail a naturalistic fallacy.

Where, then, should moral theologians find their criteria? They can refer to a variegated spectrum of anthropological options—which, however, cannot be adequately derived from the facticity of biological nature; such options transcend that facticity. Biological nature is always approached, understood, and interpreted in light of a pre-comprehension that relies on basic elements of a philosophical and theological anthropology. In addition, an autonomous process of evaluation is measured in reference to specific representations of moral values. In sum, the criterion of normative human nature as the *immediate* ground of moral action is really the result of a continuous *mediation* between different dimensions; a sort of intellectual "perichoresis" is at work here. In facing this complexity, the moral theologian is forced to reflect on the possible flexibility of the biological dimension in relation to superior personal objectives without breaking the essential unity of nature and person.

A second point of reflection for moral theology is the indisputable fact that moral judgments undergo historical evolution; awareness of the development in natural law argumentation is necessary to avoid falling prey to a thinking mode that pretends to be beyond time. The problem with this attitude is that it introduces inadequate notions of moral absolutes; moreover, too sweeping a claim in their favor may result in people's resignation when they experience the difficulty of making sense of these absolutes in relation to new cultural conditions. If history can teach us anything, it certainly teaches that false absolutes always lead to unrestrained relativism. For this reason, moral theology must carefully analyze the phenomenon of history to remain in control of new situations.

In simple fashion, the meaning of this historicity *(Geschichtlichkeit)* may identify with changes that are value-neutral: Although moral principles maintain their general validity, they receive a different application according to the historical moment and its specific challenges. What is expected for moral theology in this understanding of historicity is the art of cultural translation. In a more sophisticated conception, the theoretical work of moral theology helps us more sharply understand and define a particular issue: Its epistemic status may become more differentiated, thus requiring a broader spectrum of arguments.

Finally, in a more complete perspective, historicity means moral progress; the mind penetrates deeper in the full content of moral values, which may result in higher moral claims. One could think of the "discovery" of human rights, the humanization of penal law, or even the increasing sensitivity to the protection of life in all its forms. In all cases, moral elites always open new pathways by developing innovative competence and by bringing about, slowly but surely, a new general consciousness. Such a sense of history has nothing to do with historicism; yet it enables us to critically deal with moral claims that are raised in the name of natural law and are only presumably timeless.

At this point, we can analyze with greater precision individual areas of life such as labor, law, politics, human communication and language, marriage, family, and sexuality. In addition, we have greater awareness of the cultural variety that has evolved in the course of history and the fact that moral value systems progressively translate into general cultural patterns. The lasting contribution of natural law thought helps to maintain the consciousness of humankind's unity.

CHAPTER SEVEN

THE MORAL COMMUNITY OF COMMUNICATION AND ITS NORMS

The Variety of Moral Language

Human beings are endowed with the ability to speak. For this reason, communication of moral claims takes place mostly through the mediation of language. This situation is no contradiction to the living testimony of others; linguistic communication remains necessarily abstract and requires the clarifying and interpreting contribution of concrete experience that may better spell out the meaning of arid words. The use of language in the realm of morality is as varied as life itself. Therefore, it is difficult to reduce it to few fundamental models without doing violence to the richness and variety of interpersonal exchange itself. Yet an attempt must be made; the task awaiting moral theology is similar to that of the philosophy of language.

As always, there is a recurring distinction in the literature between scientific and prescientific language. The former is characterized by extreme precision, the exact outlining of each concept's meaning, and a groundwork leading to new definitions. Abstractness and artificiality are other typical characteristics of scientific language. This language deals only imperfectly with the many gray areas of life; intermediate tones are proscribed. Scientists must methodically detach themselves from their subjectivity, with all its dimensions, and try to be purely objective.

Prescientific language, on the other hand, is completely different. It is living and vague at the same time. The meanings of its concepts are not always sharply defined from the outset; they depend on particular circumstances, as well as the emphasis, the feelings, and the expectations of all the participants involved. This vital context becomes the hermeneutic key to prevent misunderstandings; its main characteristic is not analytic precision but fullness of meaning.

Linguistic communication in the realm of morality mirrors the distinction between scientific and prescientific language, so that both forms come to the fore. The notion of "language games" introduced by philosophers of language can be interesting to moral theologians as well. Normative language—which refers to commandments and prohibitions—represents a first language game, and it provides the arena wherein moral theologians especially concentrate. Norms require a high degree of precision because they represent the last communicative step before the concrete decision is made; therefore, we must know what their meaning is. The extent of subjective discretion, which can create misunderstandings, is to be limited as much as possible, when not completely eliminated.

In addition to the normative language there is another kind of language game, normally referred to with the word *parenesis,* or "exhortation." "Parenetic language" takes for granted the knowledge of moral obligations and—relying on this presupposition—appeals to the generosity of personal commitment. It brings forward those dimensions and motivations that may incite the person to act in an unselfish way and mobilize all the strength available to her or him.

The last type of language game is normally referred to as "narrative language"; we can even find the notion of "narrative moral theology." In this type of language, moral truths are shown and secured by reference to real-life stories and concrete models of a generally successful and meaningful life. We cannot pretend to find here the precision of normative language. Yet this imprecision is not necessarily a disadvantage because it makes room for the creative imagination of practical reason. The individual chooses what fits her or his personality and context and brings it forward in a meaningful way. Examples can inspire because the power of fascination of moral truth can be better grasped when embodied in a concrete person; her or his testimony conveys a sense of wisdom that will help others in their lives and actions.

These different language games frequently overlap with one another, especially in daily life—where necessities always combine with interests.

The Mediation of Principles and Norms

Human language moves at very different levels of abstractness. We may not be aware of this fact because we spontaneously rely on the security and spontaneity of communication without need for further reflection.

First moral principles reach the highest degree of abstraction and characterize themselves by the fact that their claim is absolute, their validity universal, and their content unchangeable. The unmistakable specificity of moral truth finds in them its purest expression. Thomas Aquinas mentions a first principle from which all others originate—namely, "do good and avoid evil" (*Summa Theol.* I-II, q. 94, a.2). This principle is immediately evident and does not require further justification: It is always and everywhere valid independent of consequences, even to the sacrifice of one's life. Unfortunately, it does not offer much help in dealing responsibly with concrete decisions because it remains vague and open to very different interpretations. Therefore, to make the communication effective, we must integrate this first principle with further mediating steps, leading to progressively greater concreteness. Indeed, philosophical and theological ethics alike face this task, which can be accomplished only through the mediation of anthropological viewpoints.

A first "co-principle" can be found in the second formulation of Kant's categorical imperative: "Act in such a way that you treat humanity, whether in your own person or in the person of another, always at the same time as an end and never simply as a means." This formulation expresses the supreme dignity of the person. Moral obligations can be regarded as a barrier against the temptation to use others as instruments. Everyone has an inalienable right to self-realization, and no one can be deprived of the opportunity of an autonomous and accomplished life. The principle of autonomy, so deeply rooted in the Western tradition, expresses this fact in a paradigmatic way. Of course, in real life one cannot avoid using others as instruments, to a certain extent; this situation is acceptable, however, if it remains only partially true and compatible with the fact that others are given a chance to take responsibility for their own lives—in other words, if it can be reconciled with the notion of a life that is meaningful and worthy of a person.

The Golden Rule is another "co-principle" that is normally found in our moral vocabulary. It comes from Greek thinking, though it also appears in the Old and New Testaments in its negative and positive formulations (Tob 4:10; Mt 7:12). It would be a gross misunderstanding to interpret the Golden Rule as a codification of egoism, however legitimate; its purpose is to synthetically formulate strict reciprocity in interpersonal relations. In this sense, the Golden Rule represents the practical application of the principle of equality: It conveys the ethical significance of the important anthropological concern according to which the fundamental equality of persons cannot be violated. Respect for the equality of the other begins in the cultivation of our thoughts and in getting rid of prejudices; indeed, all of the concrete ways in which we encounter others fall under the perspective of the Golden Rule. This process appears in the constant effort to avoid discriminations based on race, sex, religion, or ethnic origins and through a positive work of formation, as well as by means of prophylactic policy measures affecting law, society, and education.

Finally, we can find in moral language a reference to legal principles, such as "to each their own," "promises ought to be maintained," or "harm must be compensated." Beneath these principles lies the conviction that human beings are, on account of their being persons, subjects of rights (*Rechtssubject*) and bearers of subjective rights. Everyone is endowed with these rights by birth and can claim them against others while relying on the support of the legal system. Fundamental anthropological notions such as the dignity and equality of the person find their way into the law. For this reason, duties of justice have precedence over duties of love: In the former one finds the irreplaceable institutional ground upon which we can then articulate interpersonal duties of love.

Moral theology is perfectly aware of the fact that principles must be distinguished from norms. Norms fulfill an additional step toward the concrete by attempting to state explicitly the content of individual actions. They provide the precision necessary for communication to take place and decisions to be made with relative ease.

We could say that norms represent an act of solidarity on the part of the community of communication that prevents the individual from being totally left to herself or himself in the decision; she or he is thereby provided with the security of a correct and practical reference point to which the community itself attests. Norms mediate the lived experience of moral subjects and are measured by the concrete potential of their freedom. Moral theology introduces in this context the distinction between transcendental and categorial norms. Because the use of the distinction is not always univocal, further clarifications are needed.

The notion of "transcendental norms" is normally introduced with different meanings, yet they all entail a shift in emphasis with respect to the realm of principles; whereas the latter offer general orientations, the interest of transcendental norms is directed to the subjective intentionality of the agent and to securing the agent's goodness. First, transcendental norms denote the relationship with the transcendent God, manifested in the infused theological virtues of faith, hope, and love. For the Christian, every moral decision is an interpretive prolongation of this ultimate relation to God; no decision can revoke it. Second, the word *transcendental* assumes a modified meaning when it relates to life goals and ideals that transcend the present. Each person commits herself or himself during her or his life to a very particular life project that is specifically hers or his and struggles to remain faithful to this project so that she or he does not lose her or his own identity. Transcendental norms are in service of this faithfulness; insofar as they accomplish this aim properly, they claim an absolute obligation that knows no exceptions. One always presupposes, however, that a person is by definition *en route* and must spiritually accomplish her or his choice progressively, step by step. The third and final meaning of the word *transcendental* emerges in relation to the world around us. It refers to norms that connote a formal language—namely, one whose defining concepts are value laden and, as such, transcend the realm of descriptive, analytic reason. Concepts such as "lie" and "murder," for example, must be explained. Of course, we know what these terms normally mean; in situations of conflict, however, they may require additional clarifications. To secure the meaning of an action, univocal definitions must be provided in which the content of this formal language is more concretely articulated.

Categorial norms signal another expansion in the emphasis of the moral language both with reference to its epistemic interest and its regulative function. Concern for the rightness of an action, considered in its external dimension, occupies center stage; the language of values is enriched with descriptive elements to better define the phenomenon of action.

Grasping a concrete decision in its singularity is impossible; a certain degree of abstractness inevitably remains, without which communication would fall into solipsistic monologue. For this reason, a space of discretion in the application of categorial norms cannot be excluded. Everyone lays a claim on the availability of such a space, even if providing an explicit account of it is difficult. These kinds of norms cannot be understood in themselves, so to speak, by sheer reference to their formulation; hermeneutic effort is required to retrieve the profound meaning of a norm and shed light on its underlying interpretive framework, thereby enhancing the process of understanding.

First, norms must be transparent with regard to their anthropological presuppositions and framing conditions because the main purpose of categorial norms is to convey the anthropological meaning of the experience to which they refer in the first place. For example, norms concerning sexual morality can be understood only in light of the underlying interpretation and assessment of sexuality; biological structures, which by themselves remain largely ambivalent, are taken into account together with their grounding anthropological project. Ultimately, norms obligate as long as they are able to effectively protect the anthropological meaning they serve.

There is an additional element to consider: Categorial norms must respect the concrete possibilities of the individuals they address. Thus, norms cannot be imposed on individuals beyond their moral capacities. The principle of reasonableness must be respected; what surpasses the limits of reasonableness can neither be true nor obligatory. After all, God does not impose anything that is impossible (D.S. 1536). The "law of graduality" must be understood in this context (*Familiaris Consortio* 34). Such a notion appeals to a rigorous examination of conscience that can preserve the individual from the danger of cheap self-deception. A step-by-step strategy should not be excluded from the outset, however; norms cannot obscure the fact that moral action ultimately is an historical reality and needs to conform to the progressive growth of moral life. Finally, norms cannot overwhelm the physical capacity of the individual. As the moral theological tradition suggests, *ultra posse nemo tenetur:* The best norms yield to the limits of what is feasible.

At this point, we must further investigate whether the object of a given action can be divided into different components so that the obligation entailed may be met over a series of steps, or whether the obligation should be the object of a single act whose fulfillment cannot be extended along time. In the former perspective, a categorial norm entails a particular strategy in the realization of the action that leads, in the long run, to the desired result. This result should always be possible, at least when the rights of others are not being violated. There are, however, specific strategic rules to follow. First, precedence must be given to the realization of fundamental goods insofar as they are in service of higher goods. Moreover, the probability of foreseeable consequences together with the amount of human goods to be secured represent important components in defining the action's strategy. From this perspective, we must take into account the fundamental rule that harms must be avoided before we can accomplish any good. This rule of thumb cannot be disputed, although the proportion between good and bad consequences must be weighed in the particular case.

Contemporary Normative Theories

Philosophers commonly refer to the conceptual pair "deontological-teleological" when they talk about normative theories. Because this distinction is not without misunderstandings, however, we must begin with some clarifications. We encounter here two diametrically opposed normative theories that seem to entirely contradict each other. The deontological theory begins with the presupposition that moral truth is absolutely obligatory; it also takes consequences into account, yet it does so by considering them an additional but not exclusive criterion in the moral judgment of an action. The teleological theory, on the other hand, considers consequences the only criterion for the rightness of an action and the validity of a norm.

Critics of the teleological theory consider it to be another version of consequentialism and fear the surreptitious smuggling into moral theology of a mindset defined by cheap eudaimonism and technocratic pragmatism. Proponents of the theory, on the other hand, defend themselves by pointing to Christian humanism as the proper background against which the moral evaluation of an action takes place.

A look at the historic context that generated the theory may be useful. The teleological theory can be understood as a reaction against a way of thinking in moral theology that conceives *moralitas ex objecto* (morality grounded in the object of an action) according to the categories of an essentialistic metaphysics that pays no heed to the consequences. Defining an action without taking its consequences into account is impossible; one must investigate whether and to what extent the consequences, insofar as they are foreseen and therefore calculable, can make a difference in the normative definition of the action's object. Furthermore, one must assess whether the introduction of additional perspectives may provide a better grasp of the moral object in all its complexity. If so, one should be able to say without equivocation that the action's object attains its full definition *in* the consequences.

Admitting this conclusion does not imply falling into relativism—as if the goal pursued by this strategy were to assuage the significance of the norm rather than to propitiate a more adequate understanding of its meaning. On the contrary, what is at stake here is the attempt to progressively secure moral absolutes while taking their historical condition into account. Indeed, if consequences are an integral feature of the action considered in its concreteness, the moral judgment and the evaluation of the consequences must partake in the definition of the action's object. Ultimately, it may not be presumptuous to say that the contention between deontologists and teleologists is false and that it represents the result of a fundamental misunderstanding.

Norms remain abstract, to a certain degree; after all, pure concreteness cannot be mediated. For this reason, the individual addressed by the norm must take responsibility for the last step leading toward moral decision. This process happens through "concrete imperatives" that are the result not of individual arbitrariness but of thorough reflection on the ultimate meaning of a norm. Again, hermeneutic effort is required to figure out the meaning of a norm here and now, in this particular situation.

Lately, the word *epikeia* has found its way into the normative discussion. This notion, which originally belonged to the realm of human law, denotes the art of filling the existing gaps of a certain law by appealing to one's own competence to act according to the spirit rather than the letter of the law. An analogous application of the notion of *epikeia* may be possible in the context of moral norms. Of course, a moral norm cannot have any gap; nevertheless, deficiencies can creep in, in the application or the very formulation of a law. From this perspective, *epikeia* represents a work of progressive amelioration of norms that seeks to articulate, in an increasingly perfect way, their true content. *Epikeia* seeks to secure the absolute claim of morality rather than dissolving it; it does so in the form of constructive criticism.

CHAPTER EIGHT

THE JOURNEY OF MORAL DECISION

Freedom to Self-Determination

Norms must be transposed into action. The way this process takes place is worthy of deep reflection. Certainly, the model of a smooth and unproblematic extension of the norm into the materiality of space and time cannot account for the complex reality of moral action. Where do we start from, then? What appears feasible is to begin with a reflection on our understanding of freedom; we all are accustomed to the idea of freedom—much as, independent of what we mean by the word, we desire it.

In ordinary language we encounter the word *freedom* in the sense of *libertas arbitrii*—that is, freedom of choice; this term denotes the capacity to choose among different objects. Adhering to this meaning of freedom inevitably implies conceiving a moral norm in terms of external constriction, as a *gravamen libertatis*. Yet this definition may not truly convey the essence of morality. We may be able to come closer to the reality of things by changing our perspective and looking at freedom in a more profound way—namely, in terms of "essential freedom" (*Wesensfreiheit*). The latter concept is meant as a capacity to translate into action the good previously known; it denotes the power of self-determination, the daring projection of ideals, and, ultimately, the envisioning of a life goal that is generally successful and meaningful.

Obviously this notion of freedom sheds a particular light on our understanding of moral decision in terms of fulfillment of the norm. From this perspective, norms do not constrain freedom any more but liberate freedom to its full potential; they are not burden but gift.

Moreover, norms represent an act of solidarity within a moral community of communication. To make a moral decision means to find shelter within an institutional framework. Individuals are not left alone in dealing with a norm that may strain them to the limits but are accompanied by the community along the way. One important consequence of this perspective is that norms must be transparent to the community; otherwise, they contradict their very function: Instead of favoring individual flourishing, they could lead to repression and resignation, if not to cynicism.

Fundamental Option and Life Decision

Moral decision is not a one-dimensional reality; it possesses a depth that escapes the extension of a superficial outlook. Its intrinsic consistency, representing the very core of any decision, is provided by the "fundamental decision." This fundamental decision, in turn, identifies the unbending decisionality of freedom toward God as source of grace and giver of all commandments. In the fundamental decision, the person projects herself or himself toward God, finding in God her or his happiness and contentment; in this way, the person's thoughts are directed toward eternity and can sustain moral *praxis* with the continuity of a univocal dynamism.

Although the fundamental decision normally remains in the background of consciousness and, as such, precedes reflection, it is nevertheless real. The fundamental decision is not a mechanism. Gushing out of freedom, it can be destroyed by sin, slowly but surely dissolving and relinquishing its dynamism. On the other hand, when the fundamental decision is put in the condition of activating an effectual history (*Wirkungsgeschichte*), it lets each moral decision come forth as its own interpretation and ratification in the facticity of space and time.

The fundamental decision provides, then, a center of gravitation around which all moral life necessarily evolves—thus forging a reign of "pre-decision" (*Vorentscheidung*) from which every decision can profit. A pre-decision, however, can be truly effective as long as it involves a "pre-understanding" (*Vorverständnis*). Therefore, the fundamental decision also must entail a pre-understanding of the eternal perfection. Thomas Aquinas defines faith as *prelibatio visionis beatificae* (foretaste of the beatific vision); in the same vein, the fundamental decision represents the privileged hermeneutic situation in which that pre-understanding of the beatific vision finds its anthropological configuration.

A second center of gravitation for moral *praxis* is provided by the life-decision. Every person spontaneously links her or his life to a specific meaning that eventually is transposed into action during the course of her or his lifetime. This process occurs in the clearest way through the choice of a particular state of life that brings together personal and institutional dimensions in an indissoluble unity. The life decision requires that a person's entire life be totally identified with the conditions of her or his particular vocation; it so uniquely stands for the singularity of a person's life that she or he comes to recognize her or his very self *in* her or his life decision. In the Church, three states enjoy public canonical protection: marriage, priesthood, and religious life. Besides these three classical states, private forms of consecration may call for an irrevocable life choice, at least in specific cases; for example, a person may discover her or his vocation in a particular profession and bind her or his entire life to it.

A life decision does not appear like a bolt out of the blue; in fact, it may grow through a long and perhaps unknown period of preparation. Through interaction with the outside world and through personal experiences, a person develops gradually into the final form that gives public expression to her or his vocation. Once the choice is made, what follows is essentially the constant struggle to confirm the choice, to mature in it, to spiritually articulate its potential for happiness and fulfillment, and to translate it into daily life. Consequently, we could say that each concrete moral decision constitutes an interpretive extension of the life decision: A person grows toward her or his own fulfillment in light of that form (*Form*) that holds together her or his every aspect and gives expression to her or his true self. The life decision demands the investment of one's best forces, if not life itself; a life decision represents the concrete way in which the universal call to salvation finds its realization for the individual person.

The Importance of Virtue Ethics

Contemporary moral theology is sensitive to the deep dimensions of moral decisions—to the fact that they cannot be understood and evaluated in isolation or in the abstract. Moral decisions are to be regarded as expressions of their agent; they partake of a lifelong history, with all its ups and downs. Because every moral decision occurs in the larger context of a person's life experience, it inevitably reflects a particular level of personal and moral maturity.

Sensitivity to the historical dimension of a moral decision helps to explain the retrieval of the classical notion of virtue. Moral theologians are increasingly aware of the fact that actions are grounded in personal attitudes, that there exists something like permanent dispositions for whose cultivation the agent bears a particular responsibility. The retrieval of virtues, however, does not rule out the importance of normative reflection. A world that is increasingly pluralistic and centrifugal must be able to count on a system of norms that are legitimized through public consensus; otherwise, moral life would fall completely apart and be paralyzed. On the other hand, norms do not exhaust morality entirely. Stringent reflection can never account for the fullness of life in purely normative terms; new viewpoints, still in need of theoretical elaboration, will inevitably come into the picture. For this reason, it is necessary to grasp the very notions that ground norms. Depth rather than precision is required.

The attempt to work out a renewed virtue ethics must be viewed as a response to the need for a deeper ground for normative reflection. Thomas Aquinas surely provides irreplaceable insights for contemporary reflection; we cannot fail to realize how his thought is still very helpful and interesting, especially with regard to the various definitions of virtue and their reciprocal integration.

One of Aquinas's definitions of virtue is *habitus operativus boni* (an operative habit to do the good); virtue consists in a willful disposition to do the good *prompte, faciliter, delectabiliter* (readily, easily, and delightfully). One of Aquinas's interpreters, German philosopher Josef Pieper, reframes the Thomistic definition of virtue as a way of "being on the alert" (*Auf-dem-Sprung-liegen*) in the realization of the good. Virtue provides action with the certainty of a constant disposition so that particular decisions are already prepared, in a sense, by a kind of pre-decision.

Another of Aquinas's important contributions to the definition of virtue is his notion of virtue as *ultimum potentiae* (the final potency). In the virtues, moral commitment reaches its peak; the attitude of the virtuous person is anything but lukewarm mediocrity. Virtues bring forth the best in a person, and to this end, all the moral strength available to her or him is required. The task associated with virtues can be accomplished only with an entire life of dedication to the moral truth. The virtuous person knows that in the same way she or he responds to the fascination of the good, she or he enables others, who may live a life of mediocrity, to follow the attraction of the good.

Aquinas is no less aware of the fact that virtue is also a dimension of the mind, and for this dimension he speaks of a *qualitas mentis qua recte vivitur* (quality of the mind by which one lives rightly). What he means is a spiritual *connaturalitas* with the good—that is, a spiritual affinity that generates a kind of moral instinct. Of course, even the best person can make mistakes in a given situation; the presumption, however, is that the mistake remains on the periphery and sooner or later will be overcome. Finally, the virtuous person is humble enough to look forward to others' criticisms and to accept them.

Aquinas thinks as a theologian. Therefore, he naturally grounds the edifice of moral and intellectual virtues on the four "cardinal" virtues—prudence, justice, fortitude, and temperance—and regards the "infused" theological virtues of faith, hope, and love as the last measure of moral life. Because believers think of their lives within the profundity of the triune God, they can also look at their individual decisions in light of a personal history defined by the reality of faith. Nevertheless, the virtuous person cannot dispense with norms; indeed, contemporary moral theology is very careful to avoid falling into this trap. The unity of the world—which was still an obvious reality in the times of Aristotle and Aquinas—is now broken; with the advent of modernity, the person loses her or his closeness to the world and makes it a problem by retreating in the inwardness of her or his conscience and looking at reality on the basis of her or his self-consciousness.

No person can live in a pluralistic world, however, without relying on a system of rationally justified norms. Widespread confidence in the ideal of tolerance would become repressive, rather than liberating and, paradoxically, bring about the loss of personal identity. Norms are a public gesture of intellectual solidarity. Of course, norms entail duties; yet it would be a misunderstanding to regard them as oppressive impositions, or the projection of an illusory moral capacity—the objectification of moral performances that do not square with the reality of concrete life. Norms always rely on the spontaneous generosity of the person's response: They provide only a minimal framework that leaves open a space of personal discretion, particularly with regard to the degree of subjective commitment. The requirement of norms is limited to the accomplishment of the average; there still is the opportunity to do more, particularly when the individual strives to become a moral personality and develop beyond the sheer accomplishment of what is required. The realm of personal relationships is one in which the extent of individual commitment is put to the test. Virtues would miss their goal if they did not aim at the formation of the person's heart.

The Structure of Particular Decisions

Particular moral decisions are part of a larger dynamic that comprises all of the agent's presuppositions; they cannot be understood as isolated and static entities. A way of thinking that considers decisions only in their external facticity remains behind the possibility to grasp fully their very nature. Indeed, every particular decision represents a complex structure in which several dimensions are reciprocally intertwined to form an internally differentiated unity.

Motivations identify a first level in the structure of a decision. From the perspective of an empirical psychology of action—as in most of the theological tradition—motivations provide points of view that help to sharpen the meaning of a predefined obligation and facilitate its fulfillment. On the other hand, motivations acquire a different connotation from the perspective of a metaphysics of action: Here they directly mediate particular representations of moral values; in so doing, they secure the goodness of the action.

Intentions, on the other hand, plan the goal of an action and determine the strategy for achieving it. Whereas motivations account for the "goodness" of actions, intentions establish their "rightness." Through the intention, an inner action takes form that—if there are no external obstacles along the way—will be carried out as planned. In the end, the accomplishment of a concrete action and the moral judgment that measures it depend on how the action's components reciprocally integrate with one another. Therefore, a pure "ethics of intention" (*Gesinnungsethik*) remains insufficient if it is not integrated by a corresponding "ethics of responsibility" (*Verantwortungsethik*).

The tradition of moral theology has developed a subtle analysis of moral action, and contemporary discussion still draws on that reflection. There are different types of actions that cannot be reduced too hastily to a general common denominator. In particular, moral theology distinguishes between "effective" and "expressive" actions. The former intend to bring about a specific state of affairs; for this reason, strategic planning is required to secure the eventual production of the desired effect. Expressive actions, on the other hand, resist being conceived in terms of strategic calculation; they literally erupt in a spontaneous and unplanned way: One might think of actions such as laughing or crying, or expressions of approval, as well as symbolic actions. Not surprisingly, therefore, the moral evaluation must be differentiated with regard to the kind of action in question. In the case of effective actions, particular attention must be paid to rightness, whereas expressive actions must attend to the underlying intention (*Gesinnung*). As for the latter, it should be understood in an affirmative, not exclusive, sense—that is, as one element of a larger set of conditions, not the only one.

A moral action is embodied in a matrix of external conditions—starting with the obvious limitations of space and time—that reflect the very structure of the action. Actions are never of a piece: Their internal articulation is subject to fragmentation with which the agent must be able to cope. For example, in moral theology the principle of actions with double effects attempts to control an obvious situation of conflict that defines many of our decisions. Every action refers to a variety of original conditions while generating, at the other side of the action's spectrum, a chain of effects; the kind of control made possible by moral reflection in these situations can be only approximate.

More specifically, the object of the principle of double effect is an action that produces two different effects, one good and one bad, whereby the "good" is intended and the "bad" is merely tolerated. *Good* and *bad* are not to be assumed immediately in the sense of a precise moral evaluation; in fact, the two concepts refer to what could be termed "non-moral" or "pre-moral" good and evil.

Moral theology has elaborated a set of conditions that complement each other and make a moral assessment possible. First, the action must not be found morally unacceptable prior to taking all other ensuing conditions into account; if it were, every other consideration would become superfluous. Furthermore, the agent's intention must be directed only toward the good to be brought about. These two conditions are self-evident and do not require further justification. The third condition is more problematic: It requires that the evil caused not be the means for achieving the good but that the two effects arise from the action in question at the same moment (*aeque immediate*). This condition is partly entailed by the second and partly requires further justification of its own—specifically in the case in which the negative effect occurs chronologically prior to the positive one. In this case, the agent's intention decides. Finally, the fourth condition requires that a balance be struck between the good and bad effects to maintain a proportionality between the two. Here the risk involved in weighing positive and negative effects becomes apparent: Its result depends, on the one hand, on how urgent is the good to be realized and, on the other, on the lack of plausible alternatives.

An important distinction that is essential for the articulation of the theorem of double effect—which can also be found in Church documents—is the classical distinction between "direct" and "indirect" actions. Every action that is justified by the principle of double effect becomes indirect; one could think of indirect sterilization or indirect killing. All other cases identify direct actions. The difficulty, however, consists in the fact that simply looking at the way in which an action appears—that is, at its phenomenal dimension—still does not suffice in determining its morality. Only the interpretation of the meaning of various goods at stake can do that in a definitive fashion.

The theorem of "intrinsically evil" acts has been a dominant theme in the moral theological discussion for quite some time, and it can also be found in the documents of the magisterium (*Humane Vitae* 14; *Donum Vitae* II B 4). Given the ambivalence of the language, however, the meaning of *intrinsece malum* is not always clear. A first, almost evident meaning refers to the fact that an action can be good or bad according to whether it agrees with a moral norm; in this sense, the action is said to be "intrinsically" good or bad because the evaluation precedes any heteronomous human determination of law. A second meaning refers to the relation between intention and execution in the action. Indeed, certain actions in their very execution are always and everywhere bad; no good intention can possibly rescue those actions from an overall negative moral judgment. The third meaning takes into account the historicity of moral actions—on the fact that they are *always* to be morally condemned. In this last sense, intrinsically evil actions are those that under no condition are to be done: It is simply unthinkable to imagine a situation in which they would be justified.

The validity and necessity of the theorem remains undisputed within contemporary Catholic moral theology; only its more nuanced understanding is at stake. In particular, the discussion concentrates on the plausibility of a more precise analysis of the relationship between intention and execution, or between decision and circumstances. The questions remain whether, to grasp the full moral meaning of an action, the execution of the act should be kept open to its underlying intention and whether historical circumstances may bring about new points of view that ought to be considered in any moral evaluation.

CHAPTER NINE

LIFE HISTORY AS SUFFERED AND RECONCILED CONFLICT

The Inescapable Experience of Sin

Moral life bears the signs of conflict; this painful experience is common to everyone, whether Christian or not. Indeed, it is not an overstatement to say that the experience of moral conflict is a humiliating one because it brings a person to confront the evidence of her or his limitations. One could evade this embarrassing evidence by rationalizing that one's fault is only a mistake. Even if such a strategy may turn out to be successful for a limited time, however, it cannot be sustained in the long run: The moment of truth will inevitably come when every person, haunted by the disturbing and inescapable voice of her or his conscience, will have to confront her or his own sin and take responsibility for it. A person cannot undo her or his fault. She or he may let it slowly dissolve in her or his memory; with the smallest opportunity, however, the memory of the failed past will come back, freshly alive in front of the person's eyes, like the thorn in the flesh or the gauze on the wound that never heals. By incurring a certain fault, self-esteem has suffered forever; one cannot be the same person again.

No wonder then, that this experience generates a very special existential predicament. Indeed, the moral maturity of a person emerges in her or his ability to face this challenge and cope with it in a human way. This process cannot leave the moral theologian indifferent; after all, moral theology is not an academic exercise but a contribution to the life of people. The task of moral theology consists in identifying faith's contribution to the formation of a moral and religious personality. Of course, moral theology carries the heavy burden of its own history, and the moral theologian is not spared the effort to deal with it critically. Otherwise, he or she will entirely miss the challenges of the present; the underlying interest of moral theology is to keep up with the reality of people and to penetrate more deeply into the mystery of redemption.

The unfortunate legacy of a manualistic theology strongly emphasizing the notion of sin still troubles many people. Indeed, the oft-repeated criticism leveled against past moral theology—that it is based on an inflation of mortal sins—surely is not a misrepresentation of historical reality; in fact, it is right on target. Such a theology was driven by the unfortunate connection of an essentialistic metaphysics of action with moral rigorism; in the background stood the legitimate concern to provide clergy in pastoral care with practical aids for confession. There was a need to clearly evaluate the sins committed and spell out the conditions for a healing confession. For some Christians, however, this tendency led to a personal nightmare that ended in resignation or cynicism.

The problem with this theology was not so much its lack of intellectual honesty but rather its focus on the exact, downright scrupulous, determination of the gravity of each sin. Moreover, the Enlightenment's rational psychology provided the theoretical tool for judging the corresponding condition of the agent's knowledge and freedom. Manualistic theology led to a phobia of sin or, as a counterreaction, to laxism. It remains to be seen, at this point, what new elements contemporary moral theology has brought into the discussion and whether it has done so with better results than in the past.

Sin as the Sign of a Life Destiny

The notion of fundamental option discussed in chapter 8 provides a helpful framework for tackling the notion of sin in a realistic and intellectually honest fashion. We must not forget, however, that many people find the notion of sin virtually useless—especially when, as in the language of the Church, it is understood in its strict theological meaning as an offense against God. Of course, people are aware of what it means to be guilty of something, particularly in relation to themselves and to others. The link to God seems most difficult to grasp, however; thus, the notion of sin remains strictly confined within the limits of a purely immanent meaning. Moral theology bears a specific responsibility for an obvious dilemma here.

The notion of fundamental decision can provide some clarification that enables us to understand that a sinful act does not appear like a bolt out of the blue sky. It does not surprise the sinner in a sudden attack, as if the person were totally unprepared; it is always announced by a long, sometimes hidden, prehistory. The fact that this process of preparation takes place in the background of consciousness does not diminish its effectiveness. The ground for such an interior development is found in the gradual erosion and deterioration of the lived relationship with God. Emptiness finds its dwelling place in the person and, eventually, comes to express itself in corresponding deeds. Therefore the defining form of mortal sin is omission: The sinful act has already been prepared by a slow process, the silent dying of soul—that is, of the lived relationship with God. It is not an exaggeration to conclude that every sin refers back to a condition of the spirit; the sinner is truly *incurvatus in seipsum* (turned in on herself or himself): she or he has already predisposed for herself or himself an inner world of egoism that eventually finds expression in the realm of concrete deeds.

This notion of sin may appear too abstract; it must be filled with some existential content to become clear. Referring to sin as a dimension of the spirit means referring to the realm of thoughts. This realm is where every sinful act begins: at the level of inner dispositions. Patterns of thought and selective schemes prepare the ground, triggering an increasingly irreversible mechanism of self-deception so that, ultimately, one remains trapped in the spiritual prison she or he has made. As a result, it becomes increasingly difficult, and eventually impossible, for the person to find a way out.

Moral theologians are aware of the fact that each sin carries with it the mark of a specific life destiny and must be understood in relation to a person's vocation. In this sense, sin creeps in when the existential risk associated with the choice a person has made for life gets so much out of control that the choice is increasingly felt as oppressive. It is easy to foresee, at this point, how a person begins to suffer from the burden of her or his choice. She or he becomes overwhelmed with the disappointment of unfulfilled expectations, themselves already set too high. No wonder the dynamism of freedom languishes as a result, and she or he begins to yearn for alternative compensations. After all, everyone wants to get the best out of life, to be in charge of herself or himself, and to find some fulfillment; the alternative would be to let time pass by mercilessly and become a victim of destiny. In the end, the person gets caught up in an atmosphere of paralyzing fear that chokes every moral effort.

This account of a phenomenology of sin should not be mistaken for an attempt to diminish personal responsibility, as if we were more or less doomed to sin by the power of circumstances. On the contrary: Sin remains the deed of evil, born out of hatred for the good. Of course, moral theologians have to take the reality of evil very seriously; yet this requirement should not make them insensitive to the manifold existential conditions that surround sin. They must be able to distinguish between weakness and sin and search for personal responsibility where it can truly be found. The keener they are in identifying constraints on personal freedom, the more they will be able to track down the true nature of sin disguised under many different masks.

The Problem of Evaluating Sins

The reality of sin is as multifaceted as life itself. For this reason, there are clear differences in the nature and gravity of sins. This insight can be found already in the Sacred Scriptures (Job 13:26; Ps. 25:7); later, the moral theological tradition introduced the distinction between *species moralis* (moral species) and *species theologica* (theological species). The former tries to determine which moral value and which related non-moral good have been jeopardized in a specific sin; the latter, on the other hand, directly asks how a person's relationship with God has been affected. Ultimately, only "mortal" sin fully actualizes the reality of sin; "venial" sin can be termed sin only in an analogous and derivative sense. The definition of mortal sin entails both a turning away from God and a turning to a creaturely good (*Summa Theol.* III, q.86 a.4 ad 1); its conditions are full capacity of decision and gravity of matter (*materia gravis*). The fulfillment of these conditions is always approximate, at least from a theoretical point of view, and the moral judgment has to inevitably rely on an evaluation drawn from experience; the decisive condition remains the situational self-consciousness of the sinner.

Moral theology finds itself in a very difficult predicament with regard to assessing the gravity of sins because it cannot rely on a metaphysical anthropology that would provide ready-made criteria of evaluation. More specifically, the problem consists in overcoming a purely positivistic criterion. The notion of "matter," in the case of sin, is to be understood as indicative of a lived relationship with God that can hardly be determined by an objectivistic way of thinking. This last statement entails a theoretical challenge for moral theology; it calls for an anthropology articulated in the categories of philosophical personalism yielding convincing and plausible criteria for moral and theological evaluation.

Furthermore, the problem of what accounts for decision-making capacity remains to be investigated in open dialogue with the discipline of psychology. The issue here is how to determine the involvement of personal responsibility in the commission of a particular sin—a task that probably requires reading the meaning of individual acts against the backdrop of the person's life history.

In spite of these difficulties, the classical distinction between mortal and venial sins is irreplaceable. The doctrine of mortal sin gives expression to the fact that moral life, though it unfolds in time, has an eternal meaning; the here and now already decides for eternity. On the other hand, the doctrine of venial sin includes an element of hope because it is still possible to steer the rudder in a different direction. This point is important for moral pedagogy; it bespeaks the need for a prudent prophylaxis in moral life, for taking measures when the first symptoms occur and as long as the possibility of change is still there.

The Power of External Constraints

The conviction that our actions are embedded in a complex network, itself the result of diverse factors of various natures, is common. First, there are bad attitudes a person has progressively built and consolidated during the course of her or his life. These attitudes, normally called "vices," produce a negative impulse within a person that eventually affects the moral quality of particular actions. Lists of vices can be found already in Scripture (Gal 5:19); the ensuing theological tradition (Pope St. Gregory the Great and St. John Cassian) elaborated a list of "capital vices" or "capital sins": pride, envy, wrath/anger, sloth, avarice/greed, and lust. The meaning of this list is to point out situations of conflict within a person that corrode moral life and poison purity of intention and determination of the will. Once a vice has established itself, it becomes difficult to resist different temptations; the clarity of moral judgment also progressively dims. A vice is like a whirlpool: Either a person establishes a defense mechanism at the outset, or the person ends up being swallowed by a process she or he cannot control any longer.

In light of this existential predicament, moral theology cannot limit itself to the rational provision of normative claims; it has to offer concrete help for coping with real-life situations. In particular, it should be able to articulate a pedagogy that aims at reconciling the person with her or his conflicts rather than generating anger and guilt.

In addition to personal conditions, other elements affect our actions. The social and political environment represents another of the factors to take into account. A person cannot be directly responsible for the historical *milieu* in which she or he finds herself or himself, yet she or he must make the best of the situation in terms of possibilities for action. Societal and political structures set up specific constraints on freedom that may affect decisions. In this sense, Latin American liberation theology and the Church magisterium (John Paul II, *Sollicitudo rei socialis* 37) speak of the "structures of sin," which are as multifaceted as life itself. For instance, such structures could include unjust social structures that systematically preclude for many people the chance of meaningful and dignified lives. This is where the prophetic charisma of the Church is required. The Church should not limit itself to speaking up against injustice, however; it should also provide, in a constructive way, concrete alternatives that may progressively break through—and eventually heal—the determinism of structures. In particular, the level of a just social order should be addressed, as should the level of legislation. Finally, the Church should be vocal on questions of international law.

Many constraints on personal action derive from living together with others. This fact makes social interaction more difficult; moreover, it puts individuals under moral stress that negatively affects their self-esteem. In particular, people may be put in situations of cooperation with the wrong or the sin of others. Although moral theology has always been aware of the problem, the traditional approach deals with the sociological model of a consensual society *(Konsensgesellschaft)*, and does not grapple with the phenomenon of moral pluralism that characterizes modern societies. Participation in the larger dimension of sin is typified by the notion of "cooperation"—understood as cooperation with the sin of the main agent.

Within the classical paradigm, it is fairly easy to categorically exclude the possibility of a "formal cooperation" in which the person makes the sin of another her or his own by sharing in the very intentionality of the act. The axiom *peccatum non potest esse eligibile* (sin cannot be chosen for its own sake) neatly applies to the situation at stake. The moral evaluation of "material cooperation" is more problematic. The conditions required in this case take for granted that the participation in the wrong of others occurs with a good subjective intention and for serious reasons—either to secure a specific urgent good that would not be attainable otherwise or to avoid an even greater evil. The articulation of the conditions themselves owes mainly to the reflection of St. Alphonso Liguori: The closer the link between the main action in question and the act of cooperation—and the more necessary the cooperation for the main action to take place—the graver must be the reasons for tolerating the cooperation and, correlatively, the fewer the alternatives available must be. Moreover, it is never acceptable for the cooperating act to be morally bad "in itself," independent of its concatenation with the main action.

Besides these fundamental conditions, we must elaborate a clear and practical casuistry to come to terms with the issue of cooperation. More important, however, is the formation of a moral personality—the ability to distinguish situations, to recognize a sense of what is possible here and now and to appreciate how one's identity is rooted in self-esteem. A prudential prophylaxis is of particular importance; we have to recognize when to pull back to avoid being overcome by external circumstances. This awareness goes hand-in-hand with humility: Without humility, we cannot untangle, little by little, the complexity of situational constraints.

Again, the notion of moral pedagogy comes to the fore. Moral theology must ensure that the person does not give up courage when she or he finds herself or himself without any support. Perseverance and faithfulness are also necessary. They are possible only to a person endowed with strong motivations. Indeed, they are the gifts of a steadfast faith in the fact that life will have a positive outcome because it ultimately dwells in God's providence.

Life History as a History of Reconciliation

The history of the freedom of the believer is a history of progressive reconciliation in which the moral and spiritual dimensions come together. The beginning always resides in the interior realm of thoughts. We must eliminate prejudices, spontaneously recognize opportunities for selfless commitment, and vigilantly avoid falling into dangerous situations. In other words, we must create the right conditions that may, eventually, be morally fruitful. Such a task requires from the person an indefatigable, lifelong responsibility.

Moral theology is expected to be of some help in this task—first, with rigorous theological insights and second, with the critical elaboration of the results of psychological research. This assistance is necessary for moral theology to keep pace with the latest empirical findings. Of course, moral theologians are aware that by taking all the chances and risks of the interdisciplinary dialogue, they will enter intricate territory. The problems at stake are very thorny indeed. For example, what can and may be asked of a person without draining her or his moral strength in an unhealthy way, without driving her or him—no matter what the motives—to the point of resignation?

Individual actions can never be understood and evaluated in themselves—that is, independent of how they reflect one's whole life context. In this effort, the question is whether a person may, or even must—at least in the form of a provisional and hypothetical strategy—experience her or his limits to find better alternatives for her or his life. Psychology and pastoral care may need to work together to help a person find her or his own path again because sin and illness are sometimes inextricably intertwined. This relationship is legitimate when the two disciplines remain within the limits of their own competence. Of course, theologians should have the last word—but only on the condition that they do not shut off the penultimate word of human scientists, thus making their self-sufficiency a real nightmare for the person they address.

A history of reconciliation cannot avoid exhibiting the traits of compromise; in fact, doing what is good and true is inevitably subject to limits. Ultimately, the effort to overcome the constraints of an entire history of sin requires the courage to deal with fragmentation. This effort is morally legitimate as long as one honestly tries to attain what is possible here and now. On this point, Catholic moral theology leads the ecumenical dialogue. Undeniably, the meaning of the notion of "compromise" in ethics depends a great deal on the underlying theology of justification and theological anthropology. One should be aware of the fact that the same words may conceal more profound differences of thought.

CHAPTER TEN

MORAL TRUTH IN THE OPENNESS OF THE SPIRIT

Moral Truth and Theories of Truth

Moral theologians speak to the people of their time—and want to be understood by them. It is only fair, then, to require them to be intellectually open and up-to-date with the evolution of culture. In particular, moral theologians must be aware of the philosophical debate to work out a point of view that is intellectually unchallengeable. Such a demand has nothing to do with an eclectic attitude like the one characterizing moral theology in the time of the Enlightenment: it is rooted in the keen awareness that the human spirit is historically determined. Indeed, the recognition of truth's historicity cannot be played out against the absoluteness of its claim. This situation certainly holds for moral truth as well. The history of the spirit (*Geistesgeschichte*) moves toward a deeper penetration (*eindringen*) into the fullness of truth that eventually leads to the discovery of new perspectives. It is like a living mosaic whose tiles gradually come together to form an ordered whole. Intellectual patience is needed from moral theologians. They cannot feel satisfied with simplifications or, worse, give in to the appeal of improvised solutions; they must let themselves be drawn into the adventure of the spirit and travel, at least for a stretch, along the same path as philosophers who open for them the meaning of reality.

Moral theology cannot remain within the limits of a discussion about moral contents. In spite of its undeniable importance, the concern for moral norms is only one aspect—and certainly not even the most important—of moral theology's problems. The alternative would be to reduce the discipline to a casuistic application defined by the tension between general norm and individual situation. The challenges of moral theology as a science go well beyond the normative problem; they involve a reflection on the structures of thought (*Denkformen*) and their suitability for the solution of concrete issues. The typical foundational work becomes relevant at this point: It requires the capacity to look at the relevance of theoretical frameworks in the long run because they may not be of immediate use in elaborating practical solutions.

Everybody takes for granted the meaning of the word *truth* as if there were no need for any further discussion. Moral theology is no exception. Normally, it does not engage in a serious confrontation with contemporary theories of truth to expand its theoretical tools; it simply finds itself comfortable within the stream of the scholastic tradition. Unfortunately, in so doing, it precludes itself from gaining access to many contemporary problems. Lacking adequate categories, it becomes a victim of misunderstandings when it enters into a dialogue with other philosophical positions. Moral theology relies on the definition of truth it inherited from Aristotle and Aquinas: Truth is *adequatio intellectus et rem*, the conformity of the knowing intellect to its object (*De Veritate* q. I a. 1). This definition conveys an understanding of truth in terms of a formal notion expressing a relation; as such, it presupposes as its condition of possibility the ontological truth of things, itself dependent upon God's creative knowledge.

Although the foregoing definition certainly is not wrong, it must be further nuanced to avoid becoming completely irrelevant in the philosophical dialogue. Nobody denies the plausibility of the definition; in its fundamental orientation, however, it presupposes a society that is unified by a consensus (*Konsensusgesellschaft*), so it is of little help in the difficult task of establishing the meaning of truth within the context of a more complex, pluralistic society. Our society is defined by a variety of positions that are deeply divided among themselves; hence, to ground the plausibility of moral claims, we must find a more differentiated theoretical foundation.

Contemporary consensus theories of truth (Jurgen Habermas and K. O. Apel) can be very valuable in stimulating the methodological debate insofar as they try to expand, in a meaningful way, the more traditional conformation theory (*Adäquationstheorie*). Truth does not disclose itself to a purely passive knowledge; knowledge itself exercises an active, constitutive function toward truth. Knowledge has a project-like character that cannot be fully actualized by the individual but only by a collective performance. All of the participants in the dialogue bring to the table their own contributions in a spirit of freedom and fairness. Theoretical presuppositions must be disclosed to exclude positions that ground their claim on the basis of privilege or other rationally uncontrollable sources and to ensure the best results in terms of intellectual honesty and transparency.

This perspective is very important for moral theology. Because moral knowledge is structurally bound to freedom, it represents the result of a high moral performance; hence, the paradigm of empirical knowledge falls too short to adequately grasp the very essence of the moral phenomenon.

Some problems remain, however, concerning the range of truths that are open to consensual definition. The question is whether there is an intrinsic, unreconcilable tension between public and individual dimensions that forces us to take into account the disproportion that always exists between the two, thus recognizing that individuality can never be reduced within the limits of a publicly controlled operation. Otherwise, how could it be possible to vindicate the singularity of the person with her or his history of moral knowledge?

Ultimately, conceding at a metaphysical level that the person possesses a singularity of her or his own seems meaningless without recognizing the epistemological implication of this statement—namely, that the singularity of the person also means singularity of her or his moral knowledge. Here the limits in consensus theories become evident: They do not seem to be able to grasp the whole realm of truth; they remain characterized by an inevitable partiality that affects the extent of their applicability. Consensus theories have an important role to play in dealing with issues of public morality where the general question of the relation with the law is relevant. On the other hand, their applicability to the realm of individuality is bound to remain imperfect, inevitably defined by approximation.

The Integration of Different Philosophical Approaches

Moral theology is like a seismograph that is sensitive to the philosophical tendencies of the time, and moral theologians are expected to have a deep philosophical culture. Otherwise, they would not be deemed trustworthy and competent partners in the scientific dialogue; moreover, the discipline of moral theology would fall into a cultural and social ghetto. Of course, philosophies and philosophers do not pretend—as theology does—to have the final word. A discipline that makes such a claim and as a result moves in the realm of the ultimate questions cannot scorn the meaning of a penultimate reflection without undermining its own foundations. Indeed, in the past two decades there have been several systematic attempts to enrich the philosophical tools of moral theology; as a consequence, a lively exchange has ensued that can only benefit the discipline.

First, the *transcendental* approach, in its philosophical and theological version, has found its way into moral theology. The merit of this approach has been to overcome what could be termed a classical aversion to Catholic moral theology from Kantian criticism—and to have done so in a constructive way. The "Thomas-Renaissance" of neo-Scholasticism could not free itself of such a narrow attitude; "transcendental Thomism" itself was very careful in disposing completely of the historical proscription against Kant. It articulated a subject metaphysics that overcame the use of objectivistic categories without feeding the suspicion of a relativistic subjectivism. The credit belongs to Joseph Marèchal and then to Karl Rahner.

Clearly, this book is no place to discuss in further detail the plausibility of such an approach; one must realize, however, that it has unleashed within moral theology a strong and enduring history of effects (*Wirkungsgeschichte*). Transcendental Thomism represents a serious attempt to retrieve and formulate anew the fundamental project of the Thomistic tradition that was shattered by Kant. The self-consciousness of the believer plays a key role in this task. Theology is being "reduced"—in the technical sense of the word—to transcendental analysis, which is understood as self-explanation of faith-conscience that eventually articulates itself in subsequent truths of faith and their dogmatic formulation. From this perspective, transcendental analysis is embedded within the dynamism of the spirit; metaphysical and historical notions refer back to a common root. The foregoing synthesis represents the decisive interpretive key for correctly understanding moral theologians who employ the transcendental approach and rely on its method.

A clearer sensitivity to the historicity of knowledge provides sufficient basis for expanding the transcendental approach into a *hermeneutic* approach. The moral theologian is aware of standing within a long tradition that must be progressively assimilated and correctly understood in its details. This process requires the moral theologian to take into account all of the elements that have contributed to generating that tradition in the first place. One cannot deal with the different components of the tradition in a mechanical fashion and uncritically retrieve elements of the past into the present. Doing so would entail a failure to grasp the dynamic reality of the spirit and would compromise the very future of tradition.

Moral theology has learned from biblical exegesis not to concentrate exclusively on the analysis of external circumstances, whether cultural or social, but to direct its interest to the depth of intellectual presuppositions. Ultimately, the content of thought is codetermined by the formality of the mindset that generates it. An understanding of tradition can be attained when the entire spectrum of presuppositions that shape moral knowledge is taken into account. Only then can we fully grasp the meaning of moral theological assertions in their historical context.

Hermeneutics has nothing to do with relativism; its goal is not to put the absoluteness of moral claim in jeopardy but to adequately establish it. The more clearly the time-dependency of moral norms is recognized, the easier it becomes to ground their time-transcending validity. In this sense (although only indirectly), the contribution of hermeneutics is indispensable. Without it, moral theology would fall into the exaltation of uncontrolled absoluteness. The result—as a look at history clearly documents—would be not only an untenable rigorism but a remoteness from concrete life and a subsequent loss of reality.

History is more than a sequence of accidental events; it is also, and not ultimately, a dynamism of the spirit we must recognize in its particular call for the present. Consequently, hermeneutics must be understood as something more than just a method for the interpretation of texts. Indeed, moral norms are like texts whose formulation reflects the contribution of many generations; they represent the objectification of the history of the spirit that goes on. Therefore, hermeneutics can be more properly defined—much in the sense of Gadamer—as a theory of historical understanding.

Moral theology operates with both notions of hermeneutics—namely, as a method and as a theory. In so doing, it gains the status of a "human science" (*Geisteswissenschaft*) and overcomes the limits of pure casuistry. Only a moral theological hermeneutics can really control the impact of history because it brings to completion its intrinsic dynamism.

The transcendental and hermeneutic approaches are both grounded in the Continental philosophical tradition; their roots reach to the philosophy of history, German idealism, and even neo-Platonism. Moral theology ought to pay attention, however, to other currents of thought that are characteristic of Anglo-American philosophy to gain worldwide theoretical appeal; one might think here of analytic philosophy and the philosophy of language. Ludwig Wittgenstein is normally cited as the most significant representative of this tradition, although insufficient attention is paid to the entire development of his philosophy. The reference point for Wittgenstein's thinking is language, understood as the most fundamental creation of humankind and the exact copy of the surrounding world-reality. If something cannot be articulated into language, it simply does not exist. Eventually, Wittgenstein in the final phase of his thought came to pay attention and to develop the epistemic and anthropological presuppositions of language, thus regarding it more as a meaningful vehicle of transcendence and not simply the pure copy of reality.

The implications of analytic philosophy are very meaningful for moral theology. Indeed, analytic philosophy further develops and sharpens some of the tradition's fundamental concerns, particularly in reference to the precision of normative assertions (*Aussagen*). Analytic philosophers concentrate on the clarity of the concepts adopted and the rules underlying their linguistic use. Their thinking is characterized by semantic and logical rigor to ensure the internal coherence of normative systems. The latter must serve the absoluteness of moral truth and the freedom of its recognition. One cannot fail to notice here how this philosophy is unmistakably close to that of Gabriel Vasquez and to the Enlightenment in general. The best representatives of neo-Scholasticism—Viktor Cathrein may serve as an example—felt bound to scientific ideals analogous to those of the analytic tradition, with all their strengths and weaknesses.

Serving the Theological *Denkform*

These different philosophical approaches do not claim any exclusiveness for themselves; they complement each other insofar as they intend to meet different, yet equally legitimate, theoretical interests. Consequently, individual moral theologians are not forced to choose one style of thought over the others. Different philosophies may provide a specific contribution to the scientific work of theologians without denying the particularity of other theoretical accentuations. Moreover, other philosophical positions may contribute to enriching the field. One might think of many forms of personalism or, in a different direction, logical constructivism. The final goal of any philosophical option is to prepare the ground for the understanding of moral truth and the clear articulation of moral theological arguments. For the theologian, reality is always philosophically disclosed and mediated.

How can each of the aforementioned approaches contribute to a better understanding of the essence of moral truth? The transcendental approach makes clear that moral truth is bound to the self-understanding of the moral subject, which itself is transcendence-oriented and can be fully disclosed through transcendental analysis. The reference to the subject's self-understanding sets limits to an object-oriented form of thinking. Under this presupposition, one must think anew about the relationship between moral and anthropological truth; the Kantian justification of the autonomy of the moral realm must be further developed in a constructive fashion by emphasizing that its dependence on an anthropological background, far from compromising the specificity of moral truth, can bring about its full meaning. By concentrating on the importance of anthropological presuppositions, the reflection and argumentation of moral theologians can gain in clarity and consistency. Ultimately, moral truth remains in service of a meaningful and globally successful life: The moral claim represents an appeal to the person's self-esteem.

Not surprisingly, hermeneutics tries to address more precisely the question of how moral and anthropological truth relate to one another. Which anthropological presuppositions nourish the hidden roots of moral claims? Are there specific anthropological options that form the backbone of moral theological debate that may predetermine its outcome? We could call for a "depth hermeneutics" to bring back to light what is hidden. This depth hermeneutics in no way entails the arbitrariness of anthropological options, as if any confrontation on their merit were to be considered meaningless from the outset; such a position would imply that no anthropology is worthier than another— all of them being equally worthless. This attitude can only be the result of misunderstanding, and it will not fail to negatively impact any cross-cultural exchange between different anthropological perspectives. Indeed, these perspectives should be evaluated on the basis of their individual dignity, and these perspectives are also defined by ethical criteria. The link between anthropology and ethics is not like a one-way street: Each reciprocally influences the other, and their relationship need not become a vicious circle.

To be sure, moral theology is confronted, at this level, with a historic challenge concerning theology as a whole—namely, to understand what the God of Christian revelation, the One and Triune God, really means for the believer's self-understanding. Is the word *God* simply an empty formula that must remain external to the ethical debate? Are ethical insights and arguments just as convincing without reference to God?

This challenge directly concerns theologians, who cannot dodge their intellectual responsibility on this very point. They may be tempted simply to deal with the logical nature of arguments and the justification of moral norms. Yet moral theologians remain, first, theologians whose primary responsibility is to articulate the meaning of a moral claim in terms of God's call. In thinking about God and in trying to bring the reality of God to the level of language, theologians are constantly in search of a philosophical point of contact with their interlocutors. Theology's ability to exhibit a truth claim must be taken for granted; otherwise, a universal articulation of theological discourse would become impossible from the outset. Indeed, theology seeks the mediating function of philosophy (*philosophia ancilla theologiae*) to convey the specificity of its thinking.

Like analytic philosophers, moral theologians pay very close attention to the universe of linguistic communication. This statement should not be surprising: Language constitutes the first life-world (*Lebeswelt*) of the person and the vehicle of her or his communication with others. The personal exchange that actualizes the identity of those involved in the communication process—whose archetypal model *(Urbild)* is the Trinity—takes place through the mediation of language. The precision of normative language cannot choke the richness of metaphorical language; both dimensions integrate one another while responding to completely different needs of communication. Language makes communication possible not only about concrete, categorial objects but also about the human capacity to transcend the world. The act of speaking to one another must convey the intrinsic ability of language to point beyond itself. The very meaning of truthfulness pertains, first, to this very level; a truthful person encounters her or his neighbor in a dialectic of equality and respect, participates in the other's history, and meets its particular call.

CHAPTER ELEVEN

BEYOND THE HUMAN SCIENCES

Universal Dialogue

Because the human being is not pure spirit, empirical sciences have an important contribution to offer to humanity's self-understanding—in theory and practice. There is no question of falling into some kind of naturalism; failing to appreciate the specific contribution of empirical sciences and dismissing such a contribution from moral theology's interest is like forgetting reality. We could formulate the following thesis: Spiritualism always paves the way to naturalism; because the former with its intellectual categories cannot provide an adequate account of reality, it inevitably creates gaps that the natural sciences can promptly fill in—thus extending, unobstructed, their already hegemonic influence.

The dialogue with the empirical sciences is certainly not new for moral theology; indeed, regarding it as a recent achievement of modernity would only demonstrate a lack of historical consciousness. Moral theology has always been close to the empirical sciences, however different the forms of this encounter may have been. In particular, moral theology for a time was under the influence of the very notion of science shaped by the empirical sciences—to the detriment of the discipline. Moreover, truly great moral theologians have always kept pace with their times, when they were not ahead of them; they took for granted that no real conflict can exist between Christian faith and science because truth itself is one.

Of course, conflicts are quite possible, but only as conflicts between theological and scientific theories, not between theology and science as such.

Both parties have the responsibility to smooth their conflicts and even to prevent them. Theologians should constantly be reminded of Thomas Aquinas's statement that whoever intends to speak of God must know first about God's own creation. At the same time, natural scientists have a duty to be self-critical with regard to recognizing the limits of their own specific competence; scientific competence cannot stand on its own when the person and the success of her or his life are in question. Indeed, the best scientists have always thought of themselves a little bit as philosophers, as have theologians: Their effort was not only to explain but to understand nature; in so doing, they were already beyond the limits of their particular discipline.

In trying to spell out more clearly the relationship between theology and science, we should not imagine that theologians had to pay attention to everything that goes on in the natural sciences to immediately draw the consequences for their own field. This conclusion would be an obvious simplification. In the same way, natural scientists need not uncritically borrow from theologians. Indeed, what is taking place here is a more complex and riskier process of mediation that the epistemological discussion of recent decades has certainly helped us understand better. As a result, it has become clearer that, even before entering into open dialogue both disciplines have, at least surreptitiously, already borrowed elements from one another; underground channels of communication were already in existence long before they began to share arguments. After all, if theology and science had absolutely nothing in common, it would be neither possible nor understandable for them to dissent from one another.

Natural scientists inevitably rely on presuppositions that belong to the competence of other sciences, such as philosophy, cultural anthropology, religious science, and, not ultimately, theology. This reliance does not apply to the method adopted in each case. Without any doubt, the autonomy of each discipline prevails at this level. Theologians, for example, have neither a right nor the competence to question the methods or findings of other disciplines; their only choice is to accept them, unless they are recognized as an expert in the field at stake.

On the other hand, this analysis does not mean that theologians have nothing to say; in fact, they may have a lot to convey about the presuppositions with which natural sciences operate or the questions entailed by research objectives. Are the interests behind a particular research morally plausible? Do they serve the goal of a generally successful life? Finally, in cases in which those interests are not necessary, are they at least desirable?

There is a self-imposed limitation on the part of the investigator; consequences, in particular, are to be taken into account inasmuch as they are foreseeable. Ultimately, scientists and theologians stand on the same battlefield against all interests and pressures that come from a mentality—whether on the part of the individual investigator or the political system at large—that is concerned with scientific results only.

The Openness of Moral Theology

Moral theologians assume different roles when they partake in the interdisciplinary exchange. First, this exchange implies openness to learning and the awareness that scientific results can also be morally relevant. In this way, the flexibility of moral theology's underlying conception of natural law and human normative nature are tested with regard to their ability to integrate new corrections. What theologians rightly expect is to be able to improve their judgment's capacity through the empirical information they receive from scientists.

Of course, theologians do not fall into the fallacy of thinking that facts can replace the basic autonomy of practical reason or push it completely aside; indeed, the contribution of the empirical sciences remains only indirect. Yet such a contribution is so important precisely for this reason. Worldviews change slowly but steadily—which is a much more decisive factor than individual scientific results whose validity can last only for a short period. The increasing importance of a scientific worldview spawns obvious repercussions on the originally Aristotelian concept of life-world (*Lebenswelt*), a category that is constantly under the critical scrutiny of philosophical and theological ethics. Although the notion of life-world is not completely dismissed, it is put in question so that it loses, perhaps for the first time, its traditional connotation entailing both physical and metaphysical categories.

Therefore, we must elaborate a model of metaphysics at pace with contemporary sensibility, in which criteria of meaning play a dominant role and metaphysics is not pitted against physics. Moral theologians must open their conception of metaphysical nature beyond the limits of traditional categories to engage in the interdisciplinary dialogue without prejudice but in a spirit of trust. Moral theologians cannot be left alone in this task; they particularly need the help of the philosopher, who should engage the theological partner in the following question: Could some traditional positions in moral theology happen to be wrong because they rest on mistaken scientific presuppositions? In this context, one normally could point to the Aristotelian theory of human reproduction as an example, but others can easily be found.

On the other hand, we also must take a closer look at the nuances of historical judgment to rescue the honor of moral theology. Moral theology's dependence on the grip of the natural sciences, the concrete availability of alternative theories, and the possible attempt to abate false expectations ought to be taken into account and must be considered in relation to specific issues. Probably moral theology never really fell into a naturalistic fallacy because it could not have done so. It relied, however, on the presupposition of a metaphysically grounded anthropology; this circumstance, in turn, does not rule out the need to criticize the classical version of metaphysics found in the tradition. Dealing with hard empirical data presupposes some metaphysical background, as well as a readiness to question the theoretical categories employed. What is being claimed in the name of metaphysics may hide nothing but a particular ideology of physics whose unknown roots are fed by very defined anthropological presuppositions, when not by interests. The entire problematic is being decided here; clearly, then, the naturalistic fallacy is nothing but an imported pseudo-problem at whose base lies an empirically reduced ontology coupled with a naive epistemological realism.

Critical Solidarity

Moral theologians do not only learn from natural scientists; they also give something in return. In particular, they bring into the interdisciplinary dialogue viewpoints that are virtually unavailable to their interlocutors insofar as the latter remain prisoners of their own disciplines' scientific criteria. Moreover, moral theologians should not refrain from criticizing scientists when the concepts they employ transcend the expertise of their discipline—when they introduce interpretations and evaluations that derive, at best, from prejudices and by no means could be experimentally secured. Critical solidarity is required in these cases. Clearly, therefore, moral theology's fight does not have natural sciences as its target; after all, as we have seen, there is one truth only. The confrontation is directed at science's uncritical philosophy, which empowers empirical data and uses them as a weapon for its own ideological purposes. In short, the real danger is pseudo-metaphysics. This awareness gives moral theologians sufficient ground to realize that the attitude of critical solidarity has to begin with self-critique; they must work out a metaphysical basis for moral theology that is embedded within the great scholastic tradition yet does not shy away from the confrontation with contemporary critiques of metaphysics. Moral theologians and natural scientists can become responsible for the downfall of their own disciplines.

Examples of the tendency to step over the boundaries of a discipline can be found especially in the fields of psychology and bioethics. In the former, specific anthropological presuppositions clearly determine the research hypothesis as well as the interpretation and evaluation of behavioral phenomena. For example, masturbation can be given different explanations that, in turn, depend on presuppositions whose legitimacy cannot be grounded on a purely psychological basis. Ultimately, all research strategies may lead only to the validation of prejudices by means of a methodological strategy that systematically dissolves counterresults or tends to overinterpret the meaning of phenomena. Obviously, this situation is a major error in the interdisciplinary dialogue.

Moreover, we can encounter another equally grave mistake: the widespread tendency to accept unproven results at face value and to avoid verifying, in a specific case, whether one is dealing with a well-established theory or with a hypothesis that remains to be accepted by the research community. Paradoxically, moral theologians may end up having more faith in science than scientists themselves. Such a tendency reaches its peak when the philosophical elaboration and mediation of theological categories are not carried out critically; the result is the complete domination of a scientific positivism that shuts off the possibility of any further reflection.

The field of bioethics also seems to provide ample evidence of this temptation. It has become quite common to point to newly discovered biological phenomena and immediately jump to moral conclusions rather than elaborating more critically on them. Thus, the complexity of a differentiated judgment on the ethical meaning of biological phenomena surrenders to the clearest form of naturalistic fallacy whereby phenomena become immediately normative. The example of sociobiology demonstrates that a naturalistic anthropology lies beneath this attitude.

Lurking in the background there is an additional error that should not escape the attention of the scientist. In fact, one of the main merits of modern natural sciences is that it has brought about a better understanding of nature's ambivalence. Nature protects but at the same time threatens humankind; it possesses elements of undeniable order but also lacks order and is chaotic; it is both perfect and imperfect. The person is not purely passive toward nature. She or he integrates nature's hints by interpreting their meaning against the backdrop of a previously defined notion of a generally successful and good life. Therefore, the fact that things happen in a certain way in nature does not imply that the same ought to be done by the person as well.

Reference to a much-discussed example can clarify this analysis. One speaks of the "principle of abundance" in nature. Nature handles human life extravagantly, which can be seen in the high number of spontaneous abortions. Does this fact imply that, when the natural processes pass on to the person's own responsibility, the same criteria hold as for nature? More concretely, when nature fails in the pursuit of its eugenic finality, would the person be allowed to come to nature's aid and attain the finality it is unable to? Because the answer is clearly no, one can come to the following conclusion: The person's attitude toward the results of scientific research must be viewed within a larger dialectic in which natural processes give the person hints on what to do and the person, in turn, projects anthropological finalities into nature. The moral theologian's task is to project into a still-undetermined nature—in the sense described above—content-full notions of order; what is "normative" in nature, however open to subsequent corrections, will be the result of this interpretive effort. The autonomy of moral truth becomes finally evident in the fact that moral theologians can no longer count on the help of natural scientists for this task.

Learning from the Epistemological Discussion

After these reflections, the question remains whether the range of problems at stake has been fully grasped and articulated. Because that does not seem to be the case, it may be useful to take a closer look at the contemporary epistemological discussion. Through the exchange with natural scientists, moral theologians are brought back to confront the foundations of their own discipline. Indeed, these foundations may not be obvious any longer, and the fact that moral theologians are given the chance to recapture their discipline is certainly no small gain for their intellectual openness. Yet moral theologians could be tempted to fall into the mindset of logical positivism that proceeds deductively from high, unchangeable principles, or axioms, down to concrete assertions; the dominating logic is one in which the individual case is subsumed under the universal principle.

This temptation is not without historical ground. It can be detected in a large part of neo-Scholasticism's production, particularly in handbooks of the so-called Roman type; the immutable principles of "primary" natural law controlled the articulation of normative assertions of "secondary" natural law, so that the entire system distinguished itself for its immanent coherence. Here a specific scientific ideal met with a particular theory of truth—namely, the theory of coherence (*Kohärenztheorie*). At the same time, the bridge so established between primary and secondary natural law, between immutable and mutable principles, offered a theoretical tool for mediating between metaphysics and history.

The methodological weakness of this model and its need for revision emerges when we engage in a critical and constructive confrontation with Karl Popper's philosophy of science. Popper has shown, better than it had been recognized before, that scientific progress does not consist in the accumulation of new material to be eventually subsumed under formal axioms; the world of ideas provides an equally important contribution to scientific innovation. There is a continuous mediation between the history of nature (*Naturgeschichte*) and the history of the spirit (*Geistesgeschichte*). This mediation holds true for research as well; the observation of phenomena and their interpretation reciprocally condition each other.

This insight represents a particularly important suggestion for moral theology, which may learn from the epistemological discussion to pay more critical attention to the meaning of experience in the formulation of moral judgments. Of course, the concept of experience is variegated, so moral theologians must deal with it according to the different nuances of its meaning. The first meaning of experience—which is also common to natural sciences—refers to empirically verifiable phenomena; through experience, material for sensible intuitions (*Anschauungsmaterial*) is brought to practical reason. Yet moral judgment also is based on the experiences we gather in the course of life through the concrete exercise of freedom, through the challenge of different circumstances, and especially through our encounters with other persons. All of these experiences give us an opportunity to think; ultimately, experience enters moral judgment having passed through the filter of reflection and interpretation.

The results of natural sciences are ambiguous and therefore cannot immediately determine moral judgment; only moral reason can provide the additional meaning that empirical data always need to ground moral judgments. Yet moral reason as well undergoes a history of progressive discovery that brings about new points of view and may eventually lead to a different interpretation of moral norms. The critical and constructive reception of Thomas Kuhn's epistemology has helped moral theology give up its rigid notion of system and make room for a new one that is open and dynamic. We must keep in mind, however, that Kuhn, like Popper, was not only criticized—especially by his disciples—but also further developed and corrected his own views. Kuhn's notion of "paradigm shift" has had great impact—albeit in a very uncritical, simplified, and even fashionable way. Yet this uncritical acceptance should not compromise the theory's essential truth: Science is never presupposition-less; it is laden with the convictions and values of the research community that ultimately determines its progress and results. Thus, a new cultural horizon opens within which scientific problems and hypotheses are formulated and possible solutions found. Research normally takes place within an accepted paradigm that is considered valid until its explanatory potential with regard to phenomena yet to be known is exhausted. When that happens, a paradigm shift occurs whereby research moves to different foundations, and a scientific revolution takes place.

Whether moral theology shares in the Kuhnian theory or not, it nevertheless must think anew about its own foundations. We need only consider the change undergone in the recent past by natural law-based argumentation in which the notion of a *natura metaphysica et absoluta hominis* (the absolute and natural metaphysics of the human being) in the sense of Gabriel Vasquez is not to be found any more. Perhaps we must recognize that the work of moral theology also takes place within an established cultural horizon that is continuously moving and occasionally undergoes qualitative shifts. This conclusion in no way implies that we must borrow uncritically from the epistemological discussion or incorporate problems that are foreign to the discipline of moral theology; it may only prevent excessive self-confidence, which inevitably leads to sterility and eventually to the loss of truth.

CHAPTER TWELVE

THE RESPONSIBILITY FOR RIGHTS AND THE LAW

Rights as Fundamental Anthropological Category

Because moral theology bears responsibility for a generally successful and good life, there is no realm of human experience that it would not cover. Indeed, the range of its interests extends as far as life itself. Of course, tackling all of the many problems and different areas of moral theology is well beyond the scope of this introduction; therefore, one must be very selective and make choices that offer an idea of how to deal with other issues as well. Focusing particularly on the importance of rights and the law in relation to morality seems appropriate. After all, rights represent an indispensable component of a good life, without which society inevitably would sink into chaos. Moreover, all areas of life have something to do with the dimension of rights: We speak of a right to life, a right to spiritual and bodily integrity, a right to confidentiality and truth, a right to family and property; in sum, we treasure human rights as a fundamental component of society's fabric. Respect for those rights has become the grounding principle of democratic constitutions.

A fundamental anthropological conviction underlies the language of rights—namely, that the person possesses inalienable rights and that, on account of her or his personal dignity, she or he can and sometimes must claim those rights from society and the legal system. The person is a bearer of rights, which means that she or he is permanently protected from arbitrary disposal by others. Only this security allows the person to grow freely and completely. Indeed, she or he would certainly succumb without the protection of a free space that others have to respect as hers or his. Thinking about a person's dignity implies thinking about her or his rights. Rights are like an act of open solidarity with a community: The individual is not abandoned when the goods that rights protect as hers or his are threatened in any way. On the other hand, a person without rights is profoundly degraded; the lessons of history on this very point are such that nobody can afford to ignore them.

Handbooks of moral theology were criticized—especially during the period leading up to the Second Vatican Council—for having fallen into the deadly vise of the law and losing the autonomy of their own approach and methodology. The severity of this criticism does not completely square with its historical accuracy, however; the undeniable legalism of the manuals owed more to the Kantian conception of the law than to the Scholastic tradition. Because the former operates on the distinction between morality and legality, it inevitably leads to an understanding of the order of law as a purely external constraint. Not surprisingly, therefore, the gap between ethics and law became increasingly wider as a result of the aforementioned criticism: The law was identified with legalism, minimalism, and abstract and ivory-towered casuistry—in sum, with dimensions considered at odds with a healthy notion of morality that is associated with spontaneity and magnanimity.

There seems to have been a change of attitude lately, however, as a result of public discussion on so-called fundamental values (*Grundwerte*) and fundamental rights (*Grundrechte*) following the reform of criminal law. Ethics and law are no longer suspicious of one another; indeed, newly discovered opportunities of collaboration are made possible by a change toward the better in the theoretical presuppositions of both. As a result, moral theology is no longer accused of being far from reality; instead, ethics and law know and accept each other as partners that are cooperating—albeit from different perspectives—toward the same goal.

The Democratic Constitutional State

These developments raise a series of challenges for moral theology. First, we must develop an understanding of the possibilities and limits of a democratic government that is based on the rule of law. The legal system of a modern state is a system that seeks to establish and maintain order within society; it does so by balancing different interests. As a result, every citizen must accept some limits to ensure the common good. In this sense, a system of law is necessarily a compromise made possible by an attitude of reciprocal tolerance.

Correspondingly, the legislator must reckon with a series of limitations. For example, moral order and law cannot possibly overlap perfectly. Legal criteria can never grasp the whole moral truth; they inevitably remain partial. A government that wanted to legislate on every aspect of morality would become a nightmare for its citizens. The result would be paternalism and totalitarianism—not to mention the extinguishing of morality's spontaneity. For these reasons, the legislator must consider solely what is necessary for the common good.

Problems remain, however, with regard to finding moral agreement within a pluralistic system. Because all groups and all ideological positions within a society seek representation, certain concessions must be made for the sake of the whole to bring about a minimal moral consensus (*minima moralia*). Therefore, restraining expectations is necessary because government's action toward the moral consensus cannot fulfill all of its citizens' wishes in the same way. A system of law is inevitably fragmentary; it entails an appeal to individual citizens to fill in gaps in the law through personal initiative. Indeed, the legislator also expects and requires this initiative. Active co-responsibility is the fundamental virtue of a democratic constitutional state.

A constitutional state is based on a principle prescribing that each and every law be in harmony with both the letter and the spirit of the constitution. This system is intended to protect citizens. Their relation to the government is ruled by a programmatic text that the legislator (*Gesetzgeber*) is bound to respect; furthermore, any legislation becomes entirely dependent on public control.

On the other hand, the constitutional principle protects the government as well because it prevents democracy from being reduced to plebiscite. The philosophy of law commonly accepts that a constitutional order is always dependent on a pre-positive system of values. Yet such a system is not immediately evident; it is embedded within a complex social process. Therefore the legislator has no other choice than to appeal to a general moral consensus— that is, to convictions that, by their very nature, undergo change.

Collaboration between legal scholars and moral theologians is indispensable in working out a solid philosophical foundation. Such a foundation would not be possible without reference to modern theories of truth, which themselves depend on corresponding epistemologies. The consensus theory of truth plays an especially significant role because it represents the theory that most typically defines a democratic understanding of the law. Moreover, moral theologians must be familiar with modern sociological theories of law so they do not rely on obsolete theoretical models that are more appropriate for past sociological conditions; this is the price we pay for modern ideological (*weltanschauliche*) and cultural pluralism. Unquestionably, the main task is to create a moral consensus through the participation of all social components; on the other hand, the current moral theological discussion reflects the fact that improper moralization of the law must be avoided as well. The function of the juridical order is not to morally influence individuals in a direct way and thereby secure the subjective goodness of their action with the objective means of an institution. As long as morality and law relate to one another by such a strategy, the result will be an unbridled morality of power that is the sure death of any genuine morality. Indeed, morality is always linked to freedom and spontaneity; otherwise, it becomes a purely external apparatus.

The contribution of law to morality is indirect; it consists in securing (through consensus) commonly accepted criteria of right and wrong that govern the rightness of actions. Yet the law also sends out certain signals. For this reason, it exercises an implicit moral-pedagogical function by appealing to the social and political virtues of citizens. Without those virtues, there would be no life in common. The law must foster the sense of public responsibility; yet particularly in our society, with all its complexity, the danger remains that the law will degenerate to a purely technocratic apparatus. Of course, technocratic categories also have positive functions in that they allow an objectification of thinking processes—thereby protecting us from the temptation to attack and manipulate others in the name of morality. When the law incorporates a specific value system, however, it should apply that system with the greatest tolerance. Morality must remain liberating and inviting; any constraint ends up destroying its purity and strength.

Moral theologians may feel uncomfortable with this thesis; nevertheless, an attitude of moral caution is necessary. Moral theologians may cause—albeit with good intentions—exactly the opposite of what they really want. At the same time, the dangers of an overly technocratic mindset ought to be taken into consideration; indeed, the dissolution of moral criteria leaves free space for the sociologist to pontificate uncontrollably. This development would be a clear step toward another form of absolutism in which power is totally controlled by experts and the people's responsibility is progressively eliminated. Finally, naturalistic presuppositions clearly influence the notion of human beings driving such a technocratic mindset.

Co-Responsibility Instead of Obedience

The modern democratic constitutional state overcomes the classical understanding of obedience toward authority that characterizes the absolutistic state. Obedience is replaced by an attitude of active co-responsibility. The contribution of the citizens and their civic sense become central components of political life; otherwise, the basic tolerance of government would degenerate into widespread conflict.

In principle, the government respects the conscience of its people and operates from the presupposition that each citizen agrees with the programmatic statements of the constitution. As a consequence, the legislator follows the maxim never to impose anything on the people that they would not approve in conscience or that would put them in a manifest moral dilemma. Such an attitude on the government's part should be coupled with the citizens' loyalty to minimize their need, when not their duty, for conscientious objection. Citizens should abstain from hasty, simplistic judgments, especially those concerning the justice or injustice of a law. Indeed, an unjust law is really an exception because all laws must undergo many kinds of control before they are formally passed. Eventually, appeal to the supreme court remains; a democratic state always includes legal mechanisms for controlling norms: For instance, a bill could be found unconstitutional and sent back to the legislature.

In any case, the individual citizen should consider that pretending to interpret a lawful decision on one's own can easily lead to the deterioration of the legal system that people are obliged to uphold. Of course, we could have the impression that burdens are not being fairly distributed, yet the first impression may also be deceptive: What one person regards as a burden may appear to be a benefit to another—and vice versa. The citizen who feels harmed in one situation may very well be undeservedly benefited in another; public life constantly establishes a balance between these two aspects. Ultimately, citizens should treat their government fairly because governments are as good as the people let them be.

In light of these considerations, we cannot only better understand the meaning of the classical doctrine on *epikeia* within the context of a modern constitutional state but also articulate rules for its responsible application. In considering the notion of *epikeia*, Christians may be tempted to surreptitiously operate with the theoretical models of the authoritarian state; in so doing, however, they lose sight of the complex mechanisms of a democratic system and end up jeopardizing some valuable dimensions of the traditional doctrine. For example, a responsible citizen does not think and act with an attitude of self-defense toward the government, as if its intervention had to be resisted at all costs. The axiom of neo-Scholastic manuals of moral theology *finis legis non cadit sub lege* (the end of the law does not fall under the law) can no longer be entirely applied to our legal system. A contemporary understanding of *epikeia* requires an interpretation of the law that is strictly oriented to the attainment of public good; only when the law presents inevitable or unforeseen gaps can the judgment of *epikeia* be left to the individual. What is relevant for the citizen is the fundamental intention of the legislator as spelled out in the spirit and letter of the constitution. Each citizen is obligated to observe that constitution according to its strengths and possibilities. Therefore, in a particular case a citizen might go beyond the strict requirements of the law with a kind of supererogatory performance, so to speak.

The citizens' responsibility reaches even further, however. A pluralistic society runs the risk of falling apart in many uncontrollable directions; centrifugal forces can gain the upper hand, limiting moral communication to the private sphere only. This situation would clearly represent the death of morally inspired legal thought. A technocratic approach to the law would work out the gaps of morality's privatization. To prevent such an outcome, *epikeia* carefully works toward the formation of a consensus. Democracy represents an institutionalized form of dialogue in which consensus cannot be reached as in the case of empirical facts but must be progressively built. The function of social, political, and moral elites within governments, communities, and juridical cultures is essential in bringing about this goal.

The Prophetic Function of the Church

The Church's responsibility in the public sphere is great because it is entrusted with the formation of conscience. Its task is to understand how to articulate within the social arena the moral insights that grow out of faith's effective history (*Wirkungsgechichte*) and to build a consensus around them. The Church does not enjoy a privileged position; its significance can be recognized in proportion to its capacity to carry out its mission. This process may be difficult at times; it requires the Church to depend on its own credibility, especially when it engages in a confrontation that is defined by democratic rules. For this reason, the Church should not appear in the public eye as a power factor. Indeed, its weapons are the powerlessness of the Spirit, which in simplicity brings into the moral discussion the best alternatives supported by the best arguments and thus contributes to the formation of a public conscience. Of course, the Church also has a prophetic function to publicly denounce the violation of human rights, become an advocate for the poor, and provide a voice for those who do not have one of their own. In this sense, the Church becomes something like a public conscience that is supported by a long tradition. Indeed, who truly knows the human condition better than the Church?

This factor is only one side of the coin, however. The most decisive—if least visible—contribution of the Church consists in the steadfast work of formation and its persuading presence at all decisional levels where public opinion is being shaped. Obviously such an effort cannot be taken up by official Church leaders only; it necessarily relies on the collaboration of the competent laity. The best people in terms of professional expertise—such as philosophers of law, political scientists, and sociologists—should be involved in the Church's main concerns, which are always the main concerns of humankind and society as well.

This function is particularly important at the international level because the Church bears great responsibility in creating an international order of peace. In a time of increasing globalization, when the paradigm of an autonomous and self-sufficient nation-state is becoming obsolete, law and ethics must be brought together again—albeit in a new, more up-to-date fashion. Cooperation among nation-states cannot be driven by unbridled power struggles that reflect sheer economic interests; it should be based on an international moral sensibility that gives weaker countries the chance to become equal partners. The international agenda includes issues such as the environment, a moratorium on the external debts of developing countries, and the rules governing economic competition. Even more important, however, is the elaboration of strategies for the solution of conflicts; indeed, the highest goal of the Church should be to proscribe war altogether as a political tool and to favor the creation of a new atmosphere of international peace.

The democratic state is based on the principle of tolerance. It tries, at least in principle, to respect the conscience of its citizens and to expand the free space available to individuals for their personal realization. The life of any society, however, is full of constraints with which the individual has to be able to cope. Government neither can nor should regulate every aspect of the moral order. Unfortunately, too often the law cannot protect the individual from criminal assault by others.

The moral theological tradition has always been aware of this problem, which it treats under the concept of cooperation. The principles hammered out by Alphonso Liguori on the issue of cooperation are still valid. Alphonso's main concern was to protect the person's freedom without sacrificing her or his identity. Cooperation cannot be permitted when it "formally" intends the sin of another. *Peccatum non potest esse eligibile*: A person should not give up her or his own identity for the sake of moral tolerance.

Many forms of purely "material" cooperation are deemed permissible, however—for example, under conditions in which we are forced into a situation without any plausible alternative, a good end is at stake, and there is no other way to bring it about. In such a situation, we have no other choice but to work out the best strategic solution consisting of the following elements: proximity to the main action, the necessity of cooperation in securing the sinful goal, the degree and urgency of personal involvement in pursuing the goal, and the absence of plausible alternatives. The indisputable thrust in this evaluation is to eliminate, or at least reduce, all of the negative components of the act of cooperation.

A pluralistic society offers a more complicated picture on the issue of cooperation. The legislator is responsible for ensuring that the freedom of individual citizens not be overburdened by an attitude of tolerance that is impossible to bear at a personal level. Moral theology and the philosophy of law ought to pay more attention to this phenomenon. Of course, a pluralistic society offers many chances to learn; for that, it requires from all its members openness to continuous correction. Yet this openness cannot jeopardize fundamental rights, especially those of the weakest persons within society. The law must demonstrate the capacity to protect citizens by ensuring that they are free to disagree and to resist. Moreover, citizens must be able to choose to avoid situations of cooperation without having to suffer any disadvantage. The law then becomes truly a public gesture of solidarity with the conscience of the citizen; in so doing, it stands in service of the person's dignity with all its sociological presuppositions.

CONCLUSION

Catholic moral theology is as vast and variegated as the life it serves. It has reached its current form after having passed through a long and constantly changing history. An attentive person comes to the realization, however, that the development of moral theology is far from complete; in fact, it pushes into the future with all of its new challenges. Indeed, the world in which we live is becoming increasingly complicated, and this complexity has many repercussions for how we understand and do moral theology as a theological and ecclesial science.

First, there is the cross-cultural dimension of the discipline. We must develop a highly sensitive capacity of judgment to rightly appreciate and respect different cultures, with all their anthropological implications. Although we should not leave out the many differences, we must nevertheless find the basis for a consensus. Ultimately, the truth is one.

The question of God seems even more urgent, particularly in a secularized environment that pushes toward a purely categorial ethics. Moral theology requires the aid of other theological disciplines—particularly systematic and fundamental theology—to be able to rethink the relation between moral contents and God and to bring these reflections to others in a more transparent way. Indeed, the question of God is the challenge of our time; thus, moral theology cannot limit itself to the rational justification of individual moral obligations: The final and global outcome of life beyond death is at stake! By shying away from this intellectual challenge, moral theology would not only fail to meet its task, it would also surreptitiously compromise its very theological claim.

Still, there is work to do at this level. Moral theologians are called to look critically at their personal *praxis* and ask what God means in relation to their self-understanding and their vision of life. How do these questions and answers translate into concrete actions? Biographical elements inspire moral theologians in the secret hope that others will also participate in their thinking processes, thus sharing in a spiritual and existential adventure that requires utter truthfulness and humility.

Not least, moral theology requires a renewed metaphysics. Indeed, by relying uncritically on the metaphysical categories of neo-Scholasticism, the moral theological tradition has not been able to completely avoid turning metaphysical statements into normative assertions. This attitude can no longer be tolerated. Moral theology that is intellectually honest and understandable to our contemporaries does not require that we throw metaphysics overboard; it requires us to think in a way that takes human beings and their questioning as basic points of reference. The legacy of neo-Scholasticism—at least in its transcendental version—can still provide important clues about how to keep the philosophical dialogue going and how to open it beyond the limits of the tradition.

Moral theology stands at the edge between an absolutely strict science and a deeply involving existential testimony. Entering into the study of such a discipline means being prepared to bridge the gap between these two dimensions; otherwise, we miss the point. The alternative is a theory that is unable to speak to life because it limits itself to a normative discourse defined by rigor and logic. Reducing life to a system is impossible, however; life will always escape any normative category because its ground lies in the person's inwardness and her or his experience of God.

Only in the recent past has spiritual theology separated itself from moral theology and developed as an independent field. Such a separation has not been positive for either discipline; therefore, the task of regaining the spiritual dimension of moral theological discourse remains. This task cannot be accomplished, however, at the expense of a more objective analysis, as if the emphasis on the spiritual dimension of moral experience could jettison its human component. A lack of credibility would be the consequence of such an approach to moral life.

Thomas Aquinas characterizes the law of the new covenant as the grace of the Holy Spirit in the hearts of believers (*Summa Theol.* I-II 106, 1c); this grace becomes the source of an experienced and lived reality. For this reason, all moral obligations are embedded within an experience of faith. It is important to reflect on such a primordial experience, to talk about it, to allow words to convey without indiscretion the meaning of what one lives in faith.

Certainly one indication of the poverty of our times is that spirituality degenerates into something esoteric, totally escaping the possibility of any conceptual clarity. Moral theologians cannot passively stand by; their partners in dialogue must realize that in the Church dwells the divine Spirit and that life and faith-experience must be brought together in a powerful and realistic synthesis. The specific expertise of moral theology as a discipline is to articulate the extent of freedom's capacity toward the good. Its task relies on the conviction that rational argumentation must always be accompanied by the inspiration of personal testimony.

BIBLIOGRAPHY OF KLAUS DEMMER, M.S.C.
(through 2000)

Books

Jus caritatis. Zur christologischen Grundlegung der augustinischen Naturrechtslehre (Analecta Gregoriana 118) (Rome: Libreria editrice dell'Universita Gregoriana, 1961).

Sein und Gebot. Die Bedeutsamkeit des transzendentalphilosophischen Denkansatzes in der Scholastik der Gegenwart für den formalen Aufriß der Fundamentalmoral (Munich: Schöningh, 1971).

Die Lebensentscheidung. Ihre moraltheologischen Grundlagen (Munich: Schöningh, 1974).

Entscheidung und Verhängnis. Die moraltheologische Lehre von der Sünde im Licht christologischer Anthropologie (Konfessionskundliche und kontroverstheologische Studien 38) (Paderborn: Verlag Bonifacius-Druckerei, 1976).

Sittlich handeln aus Verstehen. Strukturen hermeneutisch orientierter Fundamentalmoral (Düsseldorf: Patmos-Verlag, 1980).

Deuten und handeln. Grundlagen und Grundfragen der Fundamentalmoral (Studien zur theologischen Ethik 15) (Freiburg: Herder,1985) [Italian translation: *Interpretare e agire. Fondamenti della morale cristiana* (Edizioni Paoline: Cinisello Balsamo, Italy, 1989)].

Leben in Menschenhand. Grundlagen des bioethischen Gesprächs (Studien zur theologischen Ethik 23) (Fribourg: Universitätsverlag, 1987).

Medicina salutis. Appunti per la pastorale del sacramento della riconciliazione (Rome: PUG, 1988).

Moraltheologische Methodenlehre (Studien zur theologischen Ethik 27) (Fribourg: Universitätsverlag, 1989).

Christi vestigia sequentes. Appunti di morale fondamentale (Rome: PUG, 1989).

Gebet, das zur Tat wird. Praxis der Versöhnung (Freiburg: Herder, 1989).

Zumutung aus dem Ewigen. Gedanken zum priesterlichen Zölibat (Freiburg: Herder, 1991).

Die Wahrheit leben. Theorie des Handelns (Freiburg: Herder, 1991).

Introduzione alla Teologia Morale (Casale Monferrato: Piemme, 1993).

Gottes Anspruch denken. Die Gottesfrage in der Moraltheologie (Fribourg: Universitätsverlag, 1993).

Christliche Existenz unter dem Anspruch des Rechts. Ethische Bausteine der Rechtstheologie (Studien zur theologischen Ethik 67) (Fribourg: Universitätsverlag, 1995).

Seguire le orme del Cristo. Corso di Teologia Morale fondamentale (Rome: PUG, 1996).

Medicina Salutis. La pastorale del Sacramento della Riconciliazione (Rome: PUG, 1996).

Fundamentale Theologie des Ethischen (Fribourg: Universitätsverlag, 1999).

Articles in Collections and Journals

"Moralisches Gesetz und eschatologische Vollendung," *Catholica* 16 (1962): 251–70.

"Die moraltheologische Diskussion um die Anwendung sterilisierender Medikamente. Versuch einer Übersicht," *Theologie und Glaube* 53 (1963): 415–36.

"Die hormonale Behandlung der Schwangerschaftsphobie. Ein Beitrag zu ihrer moraltheologischen Beurteilung," *Scholastik* 39 (1964): 197–219.

"Eheliche Hingabe und Zeugung," *Scholastik* 39 (1964): 528–57.

"Die moraltheologische Lehre von der 'communicatio in sacris' im Licht des II. Vatikanischen Konzils," *Scholastik* 40 (1965): 512–36.

"Glaubensgehorsam als Verpflichtung zur Wirklichkeit," *Catholica* 21 (1967): 138–57.

"Erfahrung der Sünde in der Hoffnung," *Theologie und Glaube* 57 (1967): 241–62.

"Gottes Wort und des Menschen Antwort," in *Kirchlicher Gehorsam und persönliche Freiheit,* edited by J. Tanger (Salzkotten: Meinwerk-Verlag, 1967), 55–63.

"Die religiöse Begründung des Gehorsams im Pflichtenkreis der Ordensfrau," in *Kirchlicher Gehorsam und persönliche Freiheit,* edited by J. Tanger (Salzkotten: Meinwerk-Verlag, 1967), 64–71.

"Gebet und Entscheidung. Anmerkungen zum Zeugnischarakter des priesterlichen Gebetes," *Theologie und Glaube* 58 (1968): 213–35.

"Politische Entscheidung als weltliche Glaubensentscheidung," *Catholica* 23 (1969): 38–61.

"Kirchliches Lehramt und Naturrecht," *Theologie und Glaube* 59 (1969): 191–213.

"Kirchlicher Gehorsam zwischen Autorität und Gewissen," *Theologie und Glaube* 59 (1969): 403–21.

"Mitmenschlichkeit—ein neues Wort für eine zeitgemäße Nächstenliebe?" *Bibel und Kirche* 24 (1969): 85–88.

"Kirchliche Autorität und Gewissen," *Die christliche Frau* 58 (1969): 43–50.

"Kirchlicher Gehorsam im Spannungsfeld zwischen Autorität und Gewissen," in *Protokoll über die Priestertagung vom 1–6. März auf der Hegge,* edited by Th. Wilmsen (Paderborn: Schöningh, 1969), 6–18.

"Die Ordensgelübde als Bekenntnis von Glaube, Hoffnung und Liebe," in *Dienst am Menschen,* edited by E. Wolf (Salzkotten: Meinwerk-Verlag, 1970), 36–41.

"Unverständliches Zeichen? Reflexionen über die Ordensgelübde," *Theologie und Glaube* 60 (1970): 180–203.

"Zeugnis der Armut? Theologische Überlegungen zum Gelübde der Armut," *Theologie und Glaube* 61 (1971): 413–40.

"Gelübde und Versprechen. Reflexionen über die Verpflichtungskraft der Ordensgelübde," *Theologie und Glaube* 61 (1971): 297–320.

"Kirchliches Lehramt und Naturrecht," in *Moraltheologische Probleme in der Diskussion,* edited by W. Ernst (Leipzig: Benno-Verlag, 1971), 169–88.

"Erfahrung der Sünde in der Hoffnung," in *Moraltheologische Probleme in der Diskussion,* edited by W. Ernst (Leipzig: Benno-Verlag, 1971), 227–45.

"Recht auf Leben. Moraltheologische Erwägungen zur Diskussion um §218 StGB," *Theologie und Glaube* 62 (1972): 1–23.

"Entscheidung und Kompromiß," *Gregorianum* 53 (1972): 323–51.

"Moralische Norm und theologische Anthropologie," *Gregorianum* 54 (1973): 263–305.

"Die unwiderrufliche Entscheidung. Überlegungen zur Theologie der Lebenswahl," *Internationale Katholische Zeitschrift Communio* 3 (1974): 385–98.

"Decisio irrevocabilis? Animadversiones ad problema decisionis vitae," *Periodica de re morali canonica liturgica* 63 (1974): 231–42.

"Theologia peccati anthropologice mediata," *Periodica de re morali canonica liturgica* (1975): 75–98.

"Das Verhältnis von Recht und Moral im Licht kirchlicher Dispenspraxis," *Gregorianum* 56 (1975): 681–732.

"Elementi base di un'antropologia cristiana," in *Problemi e prospettive di Teologia Morale,* edited by T. Goffi (Brescia: Queriniana, 1976), 31–74.

"Jus ecclesiae—jus gratiae. Animadversationes ad relationem inter jus canonicum et ethos christianum," *Periodica de re morali canonica liturgica* 66 (1977): 5–46.

"Wege, Umwege und Auswege in der Moraltheologie. Erwägungen zu dem gleichnamigen Buch von Franz Scholz," *Gregorianum* 58 (1977): 277–320.

"Die Weisungskompetenz des kirchlichen Lehramtes im Licht der spezifischen Perspektivierung neutestamentlicher Sittlichkeit," in *Christlich glauben und handeln. Fragen einer fundamentalen Moraltheologie in der Diskussion,* edited by K. Demmer and B. Schüller (Festschrift J. Fuchs) (Düsseldorf: Patmos-Verlag, 1977), 124–44.

"Sittlich handeln aus Erfahrung," *Gregorianum* 59 (1978): 661–90.

"Hermeneutische Probleme der Fundamentalmoral," in *Ethik im Kontext des Glaubens. Probleme—Grundsätze—Methoden* (Studien zur theologischen Ethik 3), edited by F. Compagnoni and D. Mieth (Fribourg: Universitätsverlag, 1978), 101–19.

"Christliches Ethos und Menschenrechte. Einige moraltheologische Erwägungen," *Gregorianum* 60 (1979): 453–79.

"Ethik vor dem Forum der kritischen Vernunft," *Theologische Revue* 75 (1979): 441–50.

"Die Dispens von der Lebenswahl. Rechtstheologische und moraltheologische Erwägungen," *Gregorianum* 61 (1980): 207–51.

"Tolerantia moralis et jus in ecclesia," *Periodica de re morali canonica liturgica* 69 (1980): 271–95.

"Deuten und Wählen. Vorbemerkungen zu einer moraltheologischen Handlungstheorie," *Gregorianum* 62 (1981): 231–75.

"Berufung als Geschichte mit Gott," *Ordensnachrichten* 20 (1981): 9–36.

"Cristologia e Morale. Orientamenti per una proposta sistematica," *Rivista di Teologia Morale* 13 (1981): 373–92.

"Erwägungen über den Segen der Kasuistik," *Gregorianum* 63 (1982): 133–40.

"Der Anspruch der Toleranz. Zum Thema 'Mitwirkung' in der pluralistischen Gesellschaft," *Gregorianum* 63 (1982): 701–20.

"Entscheidung zum Räteleben als Lebensentscheidung," *UISG Bulletin (Bulletin of the Female Religious Institutes of the International Union of Superiors General)* number 58 (1982): 3–22.

"Cristologia e morale: orientamenti per una proposta sistematica," in *Cristologia e morale: IX Congresso dei teologi moralisti,* proceedings of Congresso nazionale dei teologi moralisti, Nemi, April 20–23, 1981 (Bologna: EDB, 1982), 83–108.

"Sittlich handeln als Zeugnis geben," *Gregorianum* 64 (1983): 453–86.

"Si deve dire la verità al malato?" *Federazione medica* 36 (1983): 8–10.

"Liceità dell'ardita sperimentazione del trapianto cerebrale," in *Trapianto di cuore e trapianto di cervello,* edited by F. Angelini (Rome: Edizioni Orizzonte Medico, 1983), 150–69.

"Gehirnverpflanzung—ethische Implikationen," *Gregorianum* 65 (1984): 695–718.

"O homem enquanto administrador fiel da sua natureza biológica," *Internationale Katholische Zeitschrift Communio* 1 (1984): 517–32.

"Sittlicher Anspruch und Geschichtlichkeit des Verstehens," in *Heilsgeschichte und ethische Normen,* edited by H. Rotter (Quaestiones Disputatae 99) (Freiburg: Herder, 1984), 64–98.

"Identità personale e integrità biologica," in *La mente umana,* edited by F. Angelini (Rome: Edizioni Orizzonte Medico, 1984), 217–39.

"Ein Kind um jeden Preis? Anmerkungen zur laufenden Diskussion um die extrakorporale Befruchtung," *Trierer Theologische Zeitschrift* 94 (1985): 223–43.

"Geistig führen—heute. Die Ausübung von Autorität im Ordensleben," *UISG Bulletin* number 67 (1985): 19–32.

"La difesa della vita presupposto alla pace: I problemi del morire," in *La medicina per la civiltà della pace,* edited by F. Angelini (Rome: Edizioni Orizzonte Medico, 1985), 55–63.

"Vergebung empfangen und der Versöhnung dienen. Überlegungen zur Berufung des Christen auf dem Feld des Ethos," *Gregorianum* 67 (1986): 235–63.

"Das bioethische Gespräch. Initiativen katholischer Universitäten," *Herder-Korrespondenz* 40 (1986): 489–93.

"Genotecnologie e uomo: le implicazioni etiche di una sfida contemporanea," in *Nuovo genetica—uomo e società,* edited by A. Serra and G. Neri (Milano: Vita e Pensiero, 1986), 105–25.

"Coscienza e norma morale," in *Fondazione e interpretazione della norma. Contributi del XXXIX. Convegno del Centro di Studi filosofici di Gallarate,* edited by A. Rigobello (Brescia: Morcelliana, 1986), 13–50.

"Der Dienst der Versöhnung als Berufung des Christen im Kontext autonomer Sittlichkeit," in *Theorie der Sprachhandlungen und heutige Ekklesiologie. Ein philosophisch-theologisches Gespräch,* edited by P. Hünermann and R. Schaeffler (Quaestiones Disputatae 109) (Freiburg: Herder, 1987), 150–74.

"Erwägungen zum 'intrisece malum'," *Gregorianum* 68 (1987): 613–37.

"Das theologische Argument und der Paradigmenwechsel. Anmerkungen zum bioethischen Gespräch," *Freiburger Zeitschrift für Philosophie und Theologie* 34 (1987): 65–89.

"Ipotesi di ricerca sull'etica della riproduzione umana," *Giornale italiano di ostetricia e ginecologia* 9 (1987): 227–29.

"Voreheliche Enthaltsamkeit. Erwägungen zu einem pastoralen Notstand," *Theologie der Gegenwart* 31 (1988): 237–46.

"Orientierungsversuche auf schwierigem Feld. Ein Symposion über Fragen der Bioethik," *Herder-Korrespondenz* 42 (1988): 438–41.

"Une correcte gérance par l'homme de sa nature biologique," in International Federation of Catholic Universities (Fédération Internationale des Universités Catholiques) (ed.), *Débuts biologiques de la vie humaine. Des chercheurs chrétiens s'interrogent* (Paris: L'Harmattan, 1988), 261–74.

"Le génie génétique et l'homme: implications éthiques d'un défi nouveau," in International Federation of Catholic Universities (Fédération Internationale des Universités Catholiques) (ed.), *Débuts biologiques de la vie humaine. Des chercheurs chrétiens s'interrogent* (Paris: L'Harmattan, 1988), 315–31.

"Cristologia—Antropologia—Teologia Morale," in *Vaticano II. Bilancio e prospettive venticinque anni dopo (1962–1987),* edited by R. Latourelle (Assisi: Cittadella Editrice, 1988), 1035–48.

"Die Herausforderung der Moraltheologie durch die Biologie. Erwägungen zum Naturbegriff," *Gregorianum* 70 (1989): 495–519.

"Die vergessene Moralpredigt. Die Schwierigkeit ethischer Unterweisung im Gottesdienst heute," *Theologie der Gegenwart* 32 (1989): 266–76.

"Gottes Gaben—unsere Aufgabe. Überlegungen zur Erklärung von Stuttgart," *Catholica* 43 (1989): 248–67.

"Komplexe Fragen erfordern komplexe Antworten. Leistungen und Probleme heutiger Moraltheologie," *Herder-Korrespondenz* 43 (1989): 176–80.

"La persona umana—punto d'incontro di scienza e morale," *Segno* 15 (1989): 123–35.

"Die Lebensgeschichte als Versöhnungsgeschichte," *Freiburger Zeitschrift für Philosophie und Theologie* 37 (1989): 375–93.

"Das Selbstverständnis der Moraltheologie," in *Grundlagen und Probleme der heutigen Moraltheologie,* edited by W. Ernst (Leipzig: Benno-Verlag, 1989), 9–25.

"Theological argument and hermeneutics in bioethics," in *Catholic Perspectives on Medical Morals. Foundational Issues,* edited by E. Pellegrino, J. P. Langan, and J. C. Harvey (Dordrecht: Kluwer Academic Publishers, 1989), 193–222.

"Das bioethische Gespräch: Themen—Tendenzen—Fragen," in *Moraltheologisches Jahrbuch,* edited by V. Eid, A. Elsässer, and G. Hunold (Mainz: Matthias-Grünewald-Verlag, 1989), 151–68.

"Kann der Zölibat heute gelebt werden? Gedanken und Fragen aus Anlaß der Bischofssynode," *Herder-Korrespondenz* 44 (1990): 473–78.

"Natur und Person. Brennpunkte gegenwärtiger moraltheologischer Auseinandersetzung," in *Natur im ethischen Argument,* edited by B. Fraling and G. Wieland (Studien zur theologischen Ethik 31) (Fribourg: Universitätsverlag, 1990), 55–86.

"Vita umana, vita fisica, vita personale. Una prospettiva teologica," *KOS. Rivista di Scienza e Etica* (March 1990): 6–9.

"Wahrheit oder Freiheit? Gewissensfreiheit—ein Prüfstein der Wahrhaftigkeit," in *Öffnung zum Heute. Die Kirche nach dem Konzil,* edited by J. Weismayer and U. Struppe (Innsbruck: Tyrolia-Verlag, 1991).

"Das vergeistigte Glück. Gedanken zum christlichen Eudämonieverständnis," *Gregorianum* 72 (1991): 99–115.

"Il 'nuovo' nell'attuale problematica intorno allo specifico dell'etica cristiana," in *Il problema del nuovo nella teologia morale,* edited by L. Alvarez-Verdes (Rome: Editrice Rogate: Edizioni Accademia Alfonsiana, 1986), 79–98.

"Die Ehe als Berufung leben," *Theologie der Gegenwart* 35 (1992): 45–52.

"Katholische Rechtstheologie—eine Anfrage an die Moraltheologie," *Gregorianum* 73 (1992): 269–89.

"Katholische Rechtstheologie—ein Desiderat," in *Der Mensch ist der Weg der Kirche* (Festschrift J. Schasching), edited by H. Schambeck and R. Weiler (Berlin: Duncker & Humblot, 1992), 139–50.

"Moraltheologie und Kirchenrecht. Eine neue Allianz?" in *In Christus zum Leben befreit* (Festschrift B. Häring), edited by J. Römelt and R. Hidber (Freiburg: Herder, 1992), 352–66.

"Die sittliche Persönlichkeit," in *Moraltheologie im Dienst der Kirche* (Festschrift W. Ernst), edited by K. Demmer and K. H. Ducke (Leipzig: Benno-Verlag, 1992), 102–13.

"La sfida teologica del dialogo interdisciplinare," *Laurentianum* 33 (1992): 403–20.

"Statuto epistemologico della verità morale," in *Atti del Convegno,* edited by S. Ronca (Milano: Rusconi, 1992), 11–22.

"L'agire morale tra norma e coscienza," in *Atti del Convegno,* edited by S. Ronca (Milano: Rusconi, 1992), 23–34.

"Il sentire umano e il senso morale," in *Cattedra dei non credenti,* edited by Carlo Maria Martini (Milano: Rusconi, 1992), 174–78.

"Vernunftbegründung und biblische Begründung in der Ethik," *Zeitschrift für evangelische Ethik* 37 (1993): 10–21.

"Tolerancia y cooperación," *Moralia* 15 (1993): 97–108.

"Naturrecht im Zeichen der Solidarität," in *Signale der Solidarität. Wege christlicher Nord-Süd-Ethik* edited by A. Habisch and U. Pöner (Paderborn: Schöningh, 1994), 13–29.

"Optionalismus—Entscheidung und Grundentscheidung," in *Moraltheologie im Abseits? Antwort auf die Enzyklika "Veritatis Splendor,"* edited by D. Mieth (Freiburg: Herder, 1994), 69–87.

"Consensus ethics in medical genetics," in *Ethics and Human Genetics* (proceedings of second Symposium of the Council of Europe on Bioethics, Strasbourg, 30 November–2 December 1993): 78–84.

"Naturrecht und Offenbarung," in *Brennpunkt Sozialethik. Theorien, Aufgaben, Methoden,* edited by M. Heimbach-Steins, A. Lienkamp, and J. Wiemeyer (Freiburg: Herder, 1995), 29–44.

"Wahrheitsanspruch und Hermeneutik christlicher Praxis," in *Theologische Ethik im Diskurs. Eine Einführung,* edited by W. Lesch and A. Bondolfi (Tübingen: Francke, 1995), 144–62.

"Der Ursprung einer Idee," *INTAMS Review Brussels (International Academy for Marital Spirituality)* 1 (1995): 23–28.

"Die Ehe als Berufung leben," *INTAMS Review Brussels* 2 (1996): 39–62; 120–41.

"Ethische Aspekte der Reproduktionsmedizin," in *Andrologie. Grundlagen und Klinik der reproduktiven Gesundheit des Mannes,* edited by E. Nieschlag and H. M. Behre (Berlin: Springer-Verlag, 1996), 445–51.

"Anfang und Ende des Lebens—wie fließend sind die Grenzen ärztlichen Handelns?" *Gregorianum* 77 (1996): 287–307.

"Die autonome Moral—eine Anfrage an die Denkform," in *Fundamente der theologischen Ethik. Bilanz und Neuansätze,* edited by A. Holderegger (Fribourg: Universitätsverlag, 1996), 261–76.

"Ethical Aspects of Reproductive Medicine," in *Andrology: Male Reproductive Health and Dysfunction*, edited by E. Nieschlag and H. M. Behre (Berlin: Springer-Verlag, 1997), 411–17.

"Treue zwischen Faszination und Institution. Moraltheologische Überlegungen zum Gelingen und Scheitern von Lebensbindungen," *Freiburger Zeitschrift für Philosophie und Theologie* 44 (1997): 18–43.

"Ethische Wahrheit jenseits von demokratischem Konsens? Eine Herausforderung an Moraltheologie und kirchliches Lehramt," in *An-denken* (Festgabe E. Biser), edited by E. Möde et al. (Graz: Styria, 1998), 321–28.

"Ethische Wahrheit jenseits von demokratischem Konsens? Eine Herausforderung für theologische Ethik und kirchliches Lehramt," in *Ethik und Demokratie*, edited by A. Autiero (Münster: Lit., 1998), 121–40.

"Theologische Ethik in demokratischer Öffentlichkeit. Anforderungsprofile offener Identität," in *Orientierung in pluraler Gesellschaft. Ethische Perspektiven an der Zeitenschwelle* (Festschrift B. Fraling), edited by P. Fonk and U. Zelinka (Freiburg: Herder 1999), 22–40.

"Handeln als Einüben des Sterbens. Ein Kapitel theologischer Anthropologie," in *Das medizinisch assistierte Sterben. Zur Sterbehilfe aus medizinischer, ethischer, juristischer und theologischer Sicht*, edited by A. Holderegger (Freiburg: Herder, 1999), 175–91.

"Die Ehe—eine erfüllte Zeit," *INTAMS Review* 5 (1999), 163–71.

"Die Kirche—ein ethischer Denkraum," in *Zur Mission herausgefordert* (Festschrift B. Kresing), edited by Th. Schäfers, P. Schallenberg, and U. Zelinka (Paderborn: Schöningh, 1999), 75–88.

"Katholische Moraltheologie in der Polarität von Glaube und Vernunft", Freiburger Zeitschrift für Philosophie und Theologie 47 (2000), 1–23.

"Plädoyer für eine Allianz von Literur und Theologischer Ethik," Intams review 6 (2000), 34–37.

"Wahrheit und Bedeutung. Objektive Geltung im moraltheologischen Diskurs," *Gregorianum* 81 (2000), 59–99.

Articles in Dictionaries and Encyclopedias

"Ansprechbarkeit," "Heil," "Verzeihung," in *Wörterbuch christlicher Ethik*, edited by B. Stoeckle (Freiburg: Herder, 1983).

"Naturrecht IV. Katholische Kirche und Naturrecht," in *Staatslexikon der Görres-Gesellschaft*, volume 3, edited by P. Mikat and H. Krings (Freiburg: Herder, 1987).

"Gehorsam," "Gerechtigkeit," "Klugheit," "Maß," "Tapferkeit," "Toleranz," "Tugenden," *Praktisches Lexikon der Spiritualität*, edited by in C. Schütz (Freiburg: Herder, 1988).

"Eutanasia," "Opzione fondamentale," in *Nuovo Dizionario di Teologia Morale*, edited by G. Piana, F. Compagnoni, and S. Privitera (Milan: Edizioni Paoline, 1990).

"Befruchtungshilfe," "Freiheit," "Geschichtlichkeit," "Hermeneutik," "Kasuistik," "Mitwirkung," "Kompromiß," "Sünde," "Versprechen," in *Neues Lexikon der christlichen Moral,* edited by G. Virt and H. Rotter (Innsbruck: Tyrolia-Verlag, 1990).

"Christian Ethics," "Existential Ethics," "Eschatological Ethics," "Situation Ethics," "Ethics of Limit Situations," in *The New Catholic Encyclopedia* (Tokyo, 1991).

"Moraltheologie," in *Theologische Realenzyklopädie,* volume 23, edited by G. Müller (Berlin: Walter de Gruyter, 1994).

"Bontà-malizia," "Eutanasia," in *Dizionario di Bioethica,* edited by S. Leone and S. Privitera (Bologna: EDB, 1994).

"Akt II. Theologisch-ethisch," "Bittgebet II. Systematisch," "Begierde II. Theologisch-ethisch," "Entscheidung II. Theologisch-ethisch," "Freiheit V. Theologisch-ethisch," "Gebet V. Theologisch-ethisch," "Gelübde III. Theologisch-ethisch," "Lüge," "Moralsysteme," "Naturrecht II. Theologisch-ethisch," "Nüchternheit I. Theologisch-ethisch," in *Lexikon für Theologie und Kirche,* edited by W. Kasper (Freiburg: Herder, 1993–1998).

Edited Volumes

K. Demmer and B. Schüller (eds.), *Christlich glauben und handeln. Fragen einer fundamentalen Moraltheologie in der Diskussion* (Festschrift J. Fuchs) (Düsseldorf: Patmos-Verlag, 1977).

K. Demmer and K.-H. Ducke (eds.), *Moraltheologie im Dienst der Kirche* (Festschrift W. Ernst) (Erfurter theologische Studien 64) (Leipzig: Benno-Verlag, 1992).

K. Demmer and A. Brenninkmeyer (eds.), *Christian Marriage Today* (Washington, D.C.: Catholic University of America Press, 1997).

Festschriften

K. Arntz and P. Schallenberg (eds.) *Ethik zwischen Anspruch und Zuspruch. Gottesfrage und Menschenbild in der katholischen Moraltheologie* (Festschrift K. Demmer) (Studien zur theologiischen Ethik 71) (Fribourg: Universitätsverlag, 1996).

F. Furger (ed.), *Ethische Theorie praktisch. Der fundamental-moraltheologische Ansatz in Sozialethischer Entfaltung* (ICS Schriften 23) (Münster: Aschendorff 1991).

Index